THE PRESENCE
OF THE ACTOR

THE PRESENCE

Theatre Communications Group

OF THE ACTOR

Joseph Chaikin

The Presence of the Actor is published by Theatre Communications Group, Inc., 355 Lexington Ave., New York, NY 10017.

TCG gratefully acknowledges public funds from the National Endowment for the Arts, the New York State Council on the Arts and the New York City Department of Cultural Affairs in addition to the generous support of the following foundations and corporations: Alcoa Foundation; Ameritech Foundation; ARCO Foundation; AT&T Foundation; Citibank; Consolidated Edison Company of New York; Nathan Cummings Foundation; Dayton Hudson Foundation; Exxon Corporation; Ford Foundation; James Irvine Foundation; Jerome Foundation; Andrew W. Mellon Foundation; Metropolitan Life Foundation; National Broadcasting Company; Pew Charitable Trusts; Philip Morris Companies; Scherman Foundation; Shubert Foundation.

Originally published in 1972 by Atheneum.

Cover photo by Sylvia Plachy.

Title page photo by Max Waldman: *Terminal* (1971). Left to right: Tom Lillard, Paul Zimet, Shami Chaikin and Raymond Barry.

The photographs in this book are reproduced by the kind permission of the following photographers, individuals or organizations: p. 7, Phill Niblock; p. 31 and 81, Max Waldman; p. 48, The Living Theater; p. 50, Karl Bissinger; p. 63, Fred Katz; p.99, Bergh & Tornberg, Copenhagen, Denmark; p. 105, Niblock/Bough; p.114–115, Robert Frank and Ralph Gibson; p. 139, Kenneth Sklar; p. 153 and 159, Howard Gans and Claude Furones.

Chaikin, Joseph, 1935–
        The presence of the actor / Joseph Chaikin.—1st TCG ed.
        Reprint. Originally published: New York: Atheneum, 1972.
        ISBN 1-55936-030-5 (paper)
        1. Chaikin, Joseph, 1935–   . 2. Open Theater.   3. Acting.
        4. Actors—United States—Biography.   I. Title.
        PN2287.C46A3   1991
        792′.028′092—dc20   91-22915
        [B]   CIP

Cover design by The Sarabande Press

First TCG Edition, September 1991
Second Printing, January 1995
Third Printing, February 2001

For Hillary Beckett
and Jean-Claude van Itallie

A Note on the New Edition

Almost twenty years ago, on rereading *The Presence of the Actor* before it went to press, Joseph Chaikin wrote, "My life and my views change radically from one period to another. . . . In a way I wish that I could begin the book again." He resisted the impulse and we, at TCG, in republishing this seminal volume on theatrical experiment in America, have done the same. For although the intervening years have brought significant and unanticipated developments to the world, the stage, and the life and works of Joseph Chaikin, *The Presence of the Actor* remains what Chaikin always said it was, "notes from several levels of myself." It continues to inform and inspire those who consider acting to be more than an art, a craft and a profession. It helps us to see how the communal activity of making plays opens a window on our innermost needs and desires and breaks down the barriers between art and life.   —*The Publishers*

Special thanks to Bill Coco for all his help.   —*J.C.*

Foreword

Some of what follows may seem to have very little to do with acting or the theater; this may be because, for me, there is no play, novel, or movie which doesn't bring with it its own set of assumptions about people, about meaning, and often about political reality. The questions I raise with the reader, and with myself, having to do with acting, disguises, presence, and production are ones which have made up my work. With each new stage of my own training and experience, I have learned that to study or to talk about the theater is to come face to face with assumptions beyond those which I could see at first.

My work within the framework of the Open Theater has brought me into contact with many people of vast talent and ideas which have changed my life and thinking. When I encountered the plays and theories of Brecht, I began to learn dynamically to locate character within the social context, as well as the potential usefulness of the theater which up to then I hadn't begun to imagine. With Judith Malina and Julian Beck of the Living Theater I learned in a new way about the impact of the kinds of imprisonment people suffer. Whether they played to the audience as enemy or as collaborator, their inexhaustible zeal showed a degree of courage that remained unaffected by what was going on outside. Their friendship enriches me.

Through Peter Brook I saw directorial genius coupled with extravagant intelligence and talent. We have worked together in minor ways, and we have talked together.

While working on Robert Frank's film *Me and My Brother*, I spent a good deal of time with Julius Orlovsky, on whose experience the movie character I played was based. At 18 he was diagnosed a schizophrenic and he withdrew from the coherent world. He spent 13 years in one of our modern asylums. Julius had recently been released, and we stayed together for many days. I learned as much about acting and character from Julius as I have from any single experience I've had.

I have learned much from Peter Schumann's Bread and Puppet Theater, the company that impresses me the most in all of New York. Peter creates his creatures of wood and cloth and moves them about in moral and theatrical terms much as a priest uses parables in a sermon. He has discovered a special form, and creates things with it that have not existed before.

With Jerzy Grotowski I have known a poet of theater who has infused into acting a profound human meaning. His inspiration and urgent sincerity have affected me and many others. My friendship and appreciation for him have moved from severe skepticism to deep brotherhood. Still, we are on different journeys. Like those people whom I've most admired, his work and his life move and evolve. They never freeze. He lives and works with metaphors which come from deep subjective evidence.

Within the Open Theater itself, it has sometimes been possible to join with others in a common effort so intense that at the end of a project I have been unable to say which part was my work and which part belonged to someone else. The only thing I knew was that none of us were in the place we'd started from. In this company are Ray Berry, Paul Zimet, Tina Shepard, Peter Maloney, Roberta Sklar, Jean-Claude van Itallie, Sydney Schubert Walter, Joyce Aaron, my sister Shami Chaikin, Richard Peaslee, Stan Walden, Megan Terry, Lee Worley, and Susan Yankowitz.

For me, writing is difficult and inorganic work. Why does someone say one thing rather than another? Why are these and not other thoughts the ones I commit to paper? I don't understand. Still, over the last few years, I have written down some notes and thoughts about my work, myself, and about the Open Theater. These are notes, then, from several levels of myself. The only language I know how to speak is English, although I've always felt it isn't my real tongue. Until I find another, I make do.

On looking over what I have written, I feel trapped in the rules of grammar that say "he" should be used to designate either a woman or a man. I cannot think how to reinvent the grammatical form for the sake of these notes; however, I should like formally to say here that I mean both women and men when I write "the actor."

The writing of most books is a solitary act, with the author reaching down into some place within himself and working things out by himself. This book didn't happen that way; instead, it has been a cooperation between Rhea Gaisner, W.E.R. La Farge, Tony Clark, and myself. Rhea began gathering material in the summer of 1969; W.E.R. and I together expanded these rough notes, and during the summer of 1970 he gave generously of himself by blocking out and organizing the material. Throughout these stages, and particularly in the final shaping of the work, Tony Clark was with me, and his judgment and persistent persuasion have made the book possible.

THE PRESENCE
OF THE ACTOR

I

There is another world, and it is in this one.

—PAUL ELUARD

Notes on Content

Most of the people I know who are seriously interested in the theater don't really like it very much. There is the situation being played out on the stage (the play), and there is the situation of actually being in the theater—the relationship between the actors and the audience. It is this living situation that is unique to the theater, and the impulses of a new and more open theater want to manifest it.

When I go uptown and see a Broadway play, I go to see primarily the ushers, the box office, and the environment of the physical theater. *This* situation has become more present than the situation being played out on the stage.

The joy in theater comes through discovery and the capacity to discover. What limits the discoveries a person can make is the idea or image he may come to have of himself. The image can come about through his investment in his own reputation, through an

1

involvement with approval and disapproval, or through feelings of nostalgia stemming from his desire to repeat his first discoveries. In any case, when his image becomes fixed, it limits him from going on to further discoveries.

Acting is a demonstration of the self with or without a disguise. Because we live on a level drastically reduced from what we can imagine, acting promises to represent a dynamic expression of the intense life. It is a way of making testimony to what we have witnessed—a declaration of what we know and what we can imagine. One actor in his acting expresses himself and touches nothing outside of himself. Another actor, in expressing himself, touches zones of being which can potentially be recognized by anyone.

There are actors whose main interest in going into the theater is to seek a kind of flattery. This kind of seeking makes the actor, and, through him, the theater itself, vulnerable to the sensibility of the market place. Traditional acting in America has become a blend of that same kind of synthetic "feeling" and sentimentality which characterizes the Fourth of July parade, Muzak, church services, and political campaigns. Traditionally, the actor summons his sadness, anger, or enthusiasm and pumps at it to sustain an involvement with himself which passes for concern with his material. The eyes of this actor are always secretly looking into his own head. He's like a singer being moved by his own voice.

My intention is to make images into theater events, beginning simply with those which have meaning for myself and my collaborators; and at the same time renouncing the theater of critics, box office, real estate, and the conditioned public.

The critic digests the experience and hands it to the spectator to confirm his own conclusion. The spectator, conditioned to be told what to see, sees what he is told, or corrects the critic, but in any case sees in relation to the response of the critic. Unfortunately, none of this has to do with the real work of the artist.

Situations

Most of the time when we learn about acting, it is in relation to situations. In professional acting schools we play out situations of triangle love affairs; of businessmen and their families going bankrupt; of aging actresses; of people locked in boredom, etc. In our own lives all of us are involved in situations, and we often identify ourselves to ourselves in terms of the situations we find ourselves in. If you move to a strange town where you have no particular interest in what is going on, it isn't long before you become involved with the currents and stakes of those around you. The same is true of other kinds of new situations, new jobs, new friends. Situations enclose us like caves and become the walls and ceilings of our concerns.

There is no one direction in the theater today. The Living Theater, Peter Schumann's Bread and Puppet Theater, the Berliner Ensemble, Jerzy Grotowski's Polish Lab Theatre, and Joan Littlewood's theater are as different from one another as it is possible to be. They differ widely in aesthetic values and, drastically, in the relationships of their work to the lives of their creators.

The law will never make men free; it is the men who have got to make the law free. They are the lovers of law and order who observe the law when the government breaks it.

—THOREAU

Assumptions on Acting

The context of performers—that world which the play embraces—is different from one play to another. Each writer posits another level, and even within the

4

works of one writer these worlds may be quite different. An actor, no matter how he is prepared in one realm, may be quite unprepared when he approaches another. He must enter into each realm with no previous knowledge in order to discover it. An actor prepared to play in Shaw's *Saint Joan* is hardly closer to playing in Brecht's *Saint Joan of the Stockyards* than one not prepared for Shaw's work. Each play requires a whole new start. An actor can't proceed without empathy with the writer's struggle nor without an awareness of the struggle of the character he is to play.

Technique is a means to free the artist. The technique needed for the playing of a family comedy is of no use to the actor whose interests lie in performing in political theater or theater of dreams. An actor's tool is himself, but his use of himself is informed by all the things which inform his mind and body—his observations, his struggles, his nightmares, his prison, his patterns—himself as a citizen of his times and his society.

There are two ways for an actor to regard his own accomplishments: (1) he can compare present accomplishments with those of the past; and (2) he can compare himself to others.

An actor should strive to be alive to all that he can imagine to be possible. Such an actor is generated by an impulse toward an inner unity, as well as by the most intimate contacts he makes outside himself.

When we as actors are performing, we as persons are also present and the performance is a testimony of ourselves. Each role, each work, each performance changes us as persons. The actor doesn't start out with answers about living—but with wordless questions about experience. Later, as the actor advances in the process of work, the person is transformed. Through the working process, which he himself guides, the actor recreates himself.

Nothing less.

By this I don't mean that there is no difference between a stage performance and living. I mean that they are absolutely joined. The actor draws from the same source as the person who is the actor.

In former times acting simply meant putting on a disguise. When you took off the disguise, there was the old face under it. Now it's clear that the wearing of the disguise changes the person. As he takes the disguise off, his face is changed from having worn it. The stage performance informs the life performance and is informed by it.

MORE ASSUMPTIONS

Our training has been to be able to have access to the popular version of our sadness, hurt, anger, and pleasure. That's why our training has been so limited.

Shock: We live in a constant state of astonishment which we ward off by screening out so much of what bombards us . . . and focusing on a negotiable posi-

Keep Tightly Closed in a Cool Dry Place (1965): LEFT TO RIGHT, Jim Barbosa, Ron Faber, Joseph Chaikin

THE PRESENCE OF THE ACTOR

tion. An actor must in some sense be in contact with his own sense of astonishment.

"Reality" is not a fixed state.

The word "reality" comes from the Latin word *res*, which means "that which we can fathom."

Questions on the Actor's Impulse

From where is the impulse drawn?

When I make a motion with my arm, from where do I draw the energy in order to perform the motion?

If I go across the room to open the window, it's my interest in the outside that releases the energy for the walk across the room. The "impulse," in this case, is that which starts a *motion-toward*.

When an actor releases vocal sound in an exercise, where does he draw energy from? From the interest to do what the teacher told him? From the interest to do what is "good for" him?

When an actor responds to an imaginary stimulus, he himself chooses and shapes that stimulus. He has the potential for a deep contact with that stimulus, since it is privately chosen. This contact brings up energy for the actor's use. On one level or another he is given energy by his inner promptings, associations, that part of his life which is already lived.

From what part of himself is he drawing these associations as he performs? Does he draw from information and ideas of the character, the audience, and his self-image? Does he draw from a "body memory"? Does he draw his impulse from a liberated consciousness or from the same consciousness which he believes to be necessary for his daily personal safety? Does he draw from a common human source or from the contemporary bourgeois ego?

THE ACTOR MAKES A REPORT

From where in himself does the actor make his report?

Imagine a burning house:

1. You live in the house that is on fire. Even your clothes are charred as you run from the burning house.
2. You are the neighbor whose house might also have caught fire.
3. You are a passer-by who witnessed the fire by seeing someone who ran from a building while his clothes were still burning.
4. You are a journalist sent to gather information on the house which is burning.
5. You are listening to a report on the radio, which

is an account given by the journalist who covered the story of the burning house.

The actor is able to approach in himself a cosmic dread as large as his life. He is able to go from this dread to a joy so sweet that it is without limit. What the actor must not do is to cling to any internal condition as being more or less human . . . more or less theatrical . . . more or less appealing. Only then will the actor have direct access to the life that moves in him, which is as free as his breathing. And like his breathing, he doesn't cause it to happen. He doesn't contain it, and it doesn't contain him. The "act" is one of balancing between control and surrender.

During performance the actor experiences a dialectic between restraint and abandon; between the impulse and the form which expresses it; between the act and the way it is perceived by the audience. The actor is playing in present time, and comes to an unmistakable clarity that the act itself is being created and dissolved in the same instant.

An old idea of acting is that you make believe you care about things which you don't care about. To the degree that you are convincing, you are a good actor. In New York actors spend time making "rounds" for plays which they often don't care about. In between producers' offices actors go up for commercials. There the actor praises a product and testifies to the change it has made in his life. In both cases the actor is a salesman. The salesman who sells vacuum cleaners is also an actor.

Ideally, acting questions have to do with giving form to what one *does* care about. They renounce the setup which sees people as "goods." Through acting one can try to reflect the conditions of living and behaving that the revolutionary actor is trying to achieve.

On Character . . . and the Setup

We struggle with dream figures and our blows fall on living faces.

—MAURICE MERLEAU-PONTY

What is character? What do I mean by character? I mean the actor's study of a single person (not necessarily other than himself). The study of character is the study of "who" the "I" is.

In order to study character, the actor usually separates himself from others. This is the first mistake. The study of character is the study of "I" in relation to forces that join us.

We are joined to each other by forces. These forces are of two kinds. The first are observable political-social forces which move irrevocably through all of us who are alive at the same time in history. We are further joined by other forces: unanswerable questions to do with being alive at all. These second forces cannot be examined. We ask questions in words, and in response we experience a dynamic silence. In effect we are joined to each other (to all living creatures) by what we don't understand.

My early training for the theater taught me to represent other people by their stereotype—taught me, in fact, to become the stereotype. The actor's study begins with himself. In trade papers there are calls for ingenue, leading lady, character actress, male juvenile character, etc. The actor attunes himself to fit the type for which he may be cast. He eventually comes to see people outside the theater as types, just as he does for actors within the theater. Finally, a set of stereotypes is represented to the audience. This in turn is a recommendation to the types within the audience as to how they too should classify themselves.

All this supports the big setup.

Though our work at the Open Theater has been to reject these fixed ways of telling one person from another, we have found no system to replace it. Therefore, our work with character remains a study of open questions.

We find ourselves formed by the setup and may respond in one of two ways. We continue to re-create ourselves or we reinforce where we find ourselves to be. Both these ways require the same amount of energy.

How does the setup tell us to distinguish one person from another?

By the way a given person looks, sounds, and by what that person arouses in us. We know a person by his gender, his class, his profession, his love life, and his relationship to the fashions of the day.

Following this the theater actor practices a craft which reinforces the rigid stereotyping of ourselves for actor and audience alike. Meanwhile, there are zones of ourselves which have never lived yet.

In order "to make it," we need to make images of ourselves. We compose ourselves from the cultural models around us. We are programed into a status hunger. Once we have masked ourselves with the social image suitable to a type, we enter the masquerade of the setup. Even the masquerade of our ethnic and sex roles permeates our life so thoroughly that many of us are afraid to give them up. In giving them up we fear we would be giving up our identity, and even life itself.

Character as usually expressed in the theater serves to legitimize all such disguises by using as a premise that a person is contained within a set of facts, as in a sack. Each element of the societal disguise, the acceptable image, can be assessed on an almost absolute and exploitative scale of values: "It is better to be Caucasian"; "it is better to be heterosexual and male"; "it is better to be rich"; "it is better to be Protestant."

An actor who approaches character without having considered the setup falls into it.

It's within the structure of the human character to want. It's the government's and society's malfunction to determine what it is we are to want.

In Soviet and East German theater the acting student learns that the criterion for identifying "who" is the class of the character. In old French plays it's how aristocratic the character is or isn't. In religious drama it's how pure and free of sin the character is presumed to be. In many American plays it is how hung-up the character is. The study of character is not better understood by defining it—it's less understood through definition.

Our memory is like an attic which stores all the people we've ever known and we become them. The people we've known are no longer outside us.

Until we can hear the dominant voices of those ghosts whom we contain, we cannot control, to any degree, whom we are to become.

When I dream (night or day) of a particular person, it's never a photo image of that person, nor

14

is it a disguise of the person; it is, rather, the person who has become. When we sat together, we were two. When I am alone, we are both me.

There is no prepared approach to the understanding of character. The study of character, like any study where one aims to go to the root, requires a new discipline.

Since there is no existing discipline to use, an acting company must invent its own. The discipline comes about through creating exercises which bring up a common ground to those who study together. The frustration arising out of a group of people looking for an alternative way to represent the "who" is the most essential part of the development of a company. Through the frustration the group comes up against their own forms of institutionalized thinking, and the culturally dictated forces, even those fully adapted by the professional theater. The living mobile actor dealing with the prepared immobile answers becomes a dialectic toward the development of a new discipline.

What about the body of the character? All of one's past—historical and evolutionary—is contained in the body. In America many people live in their bodies like in abandoned houses, haunted with memories of when they were occupied.

All exercises must start from and return to the body in motion. To describe a living exercise on paper is no more possible than it is to write the description of a sound.

Sincerity is the consciousness of one who is caught up in his own act.

—PETER BERGER

To me Brecht's major work has synthesized an aesthetic and ethical expression of his time. Ekkehard Schall is the definitive Brechtian actor still performing in the Berliner Ensemble. As I watch him perform, I never believe he is the character by name. Nor do I believe that he is "playing himself." He performs like a double agent who has infiltrated the two worlds.

In the work of Ryszard Cieslak of the Polish Lab Theatre, there is no evidence of character in the former definition of motives and information. His work is an articulation of a common human condition. In every moment he seems aware that his "confession" is something which applies to him but not only to him.

QUESTIONS OF CHARACTER
Whom do you see when you look at me?
Whom do you think I see when I look at you?
Who or what is it that you think cannot be seen by anyone—is it still you?

16

What bits of information would be used to publicly describe you?

Does each piece of information have a value attached to it?

What system of perceiving and assessing determines that value?

Would you say that there are parts of yourself which have not lived yet?

What would bring forth the life of those parts?

The question of the "who" has the potential for giving form to the most basic conditions and experience. It has the potential for the audience to play out a recognition scene with the actor, and to help both proceed with the shared experience of living.

A good place to start is by rejecting authorities on character. In this time of high specialization not one specialist is an authority on living.

The notion of characterization as understood in our American theater is archaic and belongs with the whole hung-up attitude about the "other." Characterization formerly has been simply a set of mannerisms which disguise the actor and lend atmosphere.

In ancient Greek theater the actors wore large masks which covered their faces. The crowds were large, and these masks served to represent the main feature of the character wearing them. The characters, for the most part, were portrayed as showing one face to the world, and only in rare cases, such as Oedipus' blinding, was there a second mask for the same character.

17

When the messenger would come onto the stage, he would wear the mask of his over-all response to what he had witnessed. Furthermore, the messenger would carry the news of the significant action, which would never be performed on the stage.

A newscaster is responsible for giving one half hour of news each day at his six o'clock newscast. He goes around the city and picks up what has meaning from morning to six o'clock. The news he selects comes to represent the major news of that day. The premise he follows in deciding what has meaning is often hidden from the audience and may even be hidden from the newscaster. Still, it becomes the reference of the day's events for everyone who sees the news. Those of us who watch the news daily soon learn of the world through this newscaster and eventually take his premises as our own.

Take the psychoanalyst's standard mode of investigation. He begins with a premise, and then questions the patient or lets him talk freely about causes of his problem. He stops when he has uncovered what he considers the underlying cause. Thus his belief about underlying causes determines how far he investigates for truth, and when he thinks he has found it.

—Dr. George Weinberg

As frequently taught, characterization is an exploration of the limits of a person. The borders of the self, the outline, the silhouette, tend to be the actor's study. The conventional actor's inquiry tends to yield whatever it was designed to discover. Little remains to be discovered either about another person or about oneself. Instead, it sustains the stereotyping of people, the stereotyping of ourselves.

The path and the detour—which is which?

WHAT AM I DOING THIS FOR?

In any circumstance a person returns to the question, "What am I doing this for?" In a contest it's usually for the reward. There are events, and moments within events, which are traditionally commemorated by photographs, such as graduations, weddings, and holidays. People return to look at the photographs as recorded memory. They serve as reinforcement as to "what I am doing this for." The photograph becomes the "authentic me," and a lesser life simply goes on around and in between the occasions when the photographs are taken.

The mask which an actor wears is apt to become his face.

—PLATO

19

The temptation to play the cliché is always present. If the actor is spending a lot of energy keeping it censored, the actor may be staying inside the temptation. Sometimes if the actor plays the cliché out, he is more likely to go beyond it.

Presence on Stage

This "presence" on the stage is a quality given to some and absent from others. All of the history of the theater refers to actors who possess this "presence."

It's a quality that makes you feel as though you're standing right next to the actor, no matter where you're sitting in the theater. At the Berliner Ensemble Ekkehard Schall possesses such a quality. Some other actors with very different approaches than Schall who possess it are Ryszard Cieslak, Kim Stanley, Ruth White, and Gloria Foster. There may be nothing of this quality off stage or in any other circumstance in the life of such an actor. It's a kind of deep libidinal surrender which the performer reserves for his anonymous audience.

Schall's performance reflects the contradictions and levels which I have admired—contradictions with reference to the actor playing the character—the character that he isn't but which is contained in him.

20

These levels weave in and out and are sometimes present in combination. As I watch him, I consider my own identity in relation to my actions and my actions in relation to his character. His performance offers to the audience of Brecht's plays that perspective that makes it clear to see alternately the actor in the action and the space between the actor and the act. He offers his voice and body to the material which has been fully understood and given meaning: that is, before he embarks on his task as an actor he has come into a meaningful agreement with the main intentions of the text. It is this balancing act of abandonment and control, of intelligence and innocence, which makes his performance remarkable.

All prepared systems fail. They fail when they are applied, except as examples of a process which was significant, at some time, for someone or some group. Process is dynamic: it's the evolution that takes place during work. Systems are recorded as ground plans, not to be followed any more than rules of courtship can be followed. We can get clues from others, but our own culture and sensibility and aesthetic will lead us into a totally new kind of expression, unless we simply imitate both the process and the findings of another. The aesthetic remakes the system.

Just before a performance the actor usually has additional energy, like an electric field. It's a free-heightened space in which the actor stands. If the actor becomes at all tense, he is applying this unused energy by holding on—the way one holds onto a suitcase. The tension will form in the body of the actor as well as in the mind.

This question of tension is fundamental. I know that the opportunity of being present with a given audience is only once at a time, and I want to be there, available to the occasion. I feel myself straining and pushing when it's not intended. I'm experiencing now the imbalance of me and what I do. I'm overeager to be "understood," which is already a form of tension, a fear that if I understand what's intended, nobody else will understand it unless I shove it at them.

The actor has to allow himself—has to be available to himself—has to be able to discover and call on himself—and he also has to direct himself and guide his own process. Tension directs him to particular choices, limiting possibilities and concealing alternatives. You can't understand simply by trying—but nor can you *not* try to understand. In this sense "trying" is a form of tension.

I have a notion that what attracts people to the theater is a kind of discomfort with the limitations of life as it is lived, so we try to alter it through a model form. We present what we think is possible in society according to what is possible in the imagination. When the theater is limited to the socially possible, it is confined by the same forces which limit society.

Art creates another universe of thought and practice against and within the existing one. But in contrast to the technical universe, the artistic universe is one of illusion, semblance, Schein. *However, this semblance is resemblance to a reality which exists as the threat and promise of the established one.*

—HERBERT MARCUSE

It is comparable with a man in a room, where the door is wide open whereas the window is protected by bars; since birth I have been fascinated by the outside world and have been clutching the bars of the window; and my keenness for the image outside makes my two hands contract violently. In a sense I am not free, since this contraction prevents me from going out of the room. But in reality nothing else shuts me in but this ignorance which makes me take the imaginative vision of life for life itself; nothing shuts me in but the contraction of my two hands. I am as entitled in nature as the bear or the ape who I have been.

—PIERRE BENOIT

Prisons:

As long as there are prisons it little matters who occupies them.

—GEORGE BERNARD SHAW

Anyone in prison believes that outside his walls is a free world.

—BERTRAND RUSSELL

Whenever there is too much discipline it is invariably being imposed by someone else.

—CHOGYAM TRUNGPA

People are so swamped by the conditions of modern life that they do not really believe that these evils are human artifacts and could be otherwise.

—PAUL GOODMAN

Individual sanity is not immune to mass insanity.

—ALDOUS HUXLEY

This country, with its institutions, belongs to the people who inhabit it. Whenever they shall grow

*weary of the existing Government, they can exercise
their constitutional right of amending it, or their
revolutionary right to dismember or overthrow it.*

—ABRAHAM LINCOLN

The theater, insofar as people are serious in it,
seems to be looking for a place where it is not a dupli-
cation of life. It exists not just to make a mirror of
life, but to represent a kind of realm just as certainly
as music is a realm. But because the theater involves
behavior and language, it can't be completely separate from the situational world, as music can. But
much passes between people in the theater which is
intuitive and not at all concrete, having nothing to do
with data. It's like marking off territories in which
to enter together.

I think that each step of acting requires an actor
to return to a conscious awareness of what he is doing.
Most of his creative work is done in that dream life,
and this sometimes requires that the actor rest, and
let the image move itself.

There are zones in us which know more than we
think they do. The secret is in knowing how to listen
to them.

We are born little animals unable to care for ourselves and crying with anger at being alive. Our
voices become what is necessary to speak English

with. Our wishes are modified by what seems possible to attain. The whole spectrum of imagination humbles itself to what is available to understand. We must unmask and be vulnerable all over again.

There is that level on which we live where we deal with obtainable information and assumptions and we exchange with one another the currency of data. Then there is that other level, from which we also act, where there is no possibility of fixing conclusions or exchanging facts. In that creative stage the actor is in a bafflement which has no sophistication and no direct information. He has suspended his personal protective armor and is without what we know to be an organized identity. But it is on this level that it is most possible to meet him.

II

We returned from Europe in the summer of 1968, after performing *The Serpent* on a tour of European cities. The tour introduced many problems we hadn't foreseen, and much adventure we hadn't expected. After a holiday interim we were to meet again and start the next year's work, which meant finishing the still unfinished *Serpent* and approaching problems that we had been putting off.

We had committed ourselves to performing *The Serpent* in America, and when we resumed rehearsals, we found ourselves estranged from the piece and unable to recapture our original enthusiasm. Three actors quit. The rest of us wanted to examine the problem and understand what had happened to this work that we had recently been so attached to. We looked at it as though it were a script by somebody we didn't know, when it was actually a work that we had created together with Jean-Claude van Itallie.

A company of actors—in relation to the work that they are performing—is a community. We had no relationship to one another, and the personal tensions which had come out during the tour of Europe were our main preoccupations. We started from scratch, from the procession which begins the piece, and then examined and re-examined and re-examined our attitudes to the audience and to the material. Only when we finally began to examine our process of examining were we able to alter our approach to a more creative one, and only at the point where we fully gave up and let the production collapse were we able to begin to build. We slowly did exercises in and around the material and began to reconstruct the work. This time we reconstructed it in a much more formal way because it was much clearer what the intentions were to be. In trying to do everything, a kind of chaos had come about and the image had become drowned by all the associations and overlay. There are many things in *The Serpent* which are still unsolved—in fact, I don't remember being part of any ambitious work which has seemed to me solved. But through this new process of working on the same piece, we rediscovered our relationship to it and consequently to one another. The personal hang-ups always take precedence, unless the ensemble is fully focused on the work. Then when we are fully focused, the process of work suggests itself through the involvement, and the actors become "theater workers." In the work from *The Serpent* in 1968 through *Terminal* and *Mutations* in 1971, my own function as director was in partnership with Roberta Sklar, a partnership that began midway in the preparation of *The Serpent,* around January 1968, and ending in the winter of 1972.

Notes on Terminal *—Winter 1969*

We began with an idea of trying to confront the dread of dying. As we started going into our own fantasy and imagining our own impermanence, we began to think that there was a conspiracy to keep us from being aware that we were, in fact, part of nature: that we are alive now, and one day we will not be. As we felt through this dread of personal extinction and society's disguising of the process, we looked for a tale around which we could explore images and ideas.

We invited an embalmer to talk to us about the process of embalming the body. He described that the body is first drained of the dead blood, embalming fluid is put into the body through the orifices, a number of internal organs are taken out and up-holsterylike stuffing is put in their place, the lips and the eyes are sewed shut so that they will not open, and then cosmetics are applied to give a lifelike look to the deceased. In other words everything is done so that the appearance of the dead body will be agreeable to the living. The embalmer explained that this was the law. This visit helped to confirm the idea of disguising death and the process of dying so as to keep us still farther from our own nature.

"We come upon the dying to call upon the dead." We tried many routes to call up the dead: we invented some, and we studied procedures used by people who believe in invocation. What we chose finally was to knock on the door of the dead by tapping with the feet on the floor, the door of the dead. There is no ground where underfoot—below the wood, below the stone—are not the bones of someone who once lived. The guides invite the dead below the stage floor to come through and speak through the dying.

Then the dying dance on the graves of the dead. They knock on the doors of their graves. They say: "Let the dead come through, and let it begin with me." Then the dying make their bodies available for the entrance of the dead and they make their voices available, and the dead enter the bodies of the dying. Then the dead come through and speak. The idea is that the dead have already lived through our arguments, so they can see in retrospect.

We went through many detours and revisions as we evolved *Terminal*. Several themes had to be dropped because we couldn't find a way to articulate them.

During this time we also worked on the idea of

Terminal (1971): LEFT TO RIGHT, Shami Chaikin, Raymond Barry

the soul, and especially on the primitive notion of
its relationship with the body. We studied James
George Frazer's idea that "the animal inside the animal, the man inside the man, is the soul." We worked
on the notions of the soul's (Latin, *anima*) escape
from the body through its natural openings, and on
the primitive idea that the soul of a sleeper wanders
from his body and may fall into danger. We also ex-
perimented with the idea of the pregnant dying. We
tried a story of a woman who was the last of a race
which was almost extinct. Someone would be found
to impregnate her, but all the while she would be
dying: through that one body life is moving in and
life moving out: the baby is coming into life and the
woman is going into death.

*Death is always inside us, like a pregnant woman
carrying a dead baby.*

—RILKE

At essential points during the working out of the
material we talked to Joseph Campbell. He came to a
workshop and spoke to us about the mythology of
passage from the living to the dead place. He referred
to Egyptian, Tibetan, Zoroastrian, and other sources.
He recommended that as we worked on this material,
rather than basing it on an existing mythology,

we might have tried to create our own. He referred to mythology as personifications of states of mind and projections of fears and wishes. He referred to religious stories as poems using symbols, the symbols being signs of those things which one could not otherwise find a way to talk about.

III

Notes on Brecht

*The problem holds for all art, and it is a vast one
. . . which can be expressed so: How can the theatre
be both instructive and entertaining? How can it be
divorced from spiritual dope traffic and turned from
a home of illusions to a home of experience? How can
the unfree, ignorant man of our century, with his
thirst for freedom and his hunger for knowledge,
how can the tortured and heroic, abused and in-
genious, changeable and world-changing man of this
great and ghastly century obtain his own theatre,
which will help him to master the world and himself?*

—BRECHT

Theories and systems on paper are seldom what
they are when they are an active process. Once on
paper they get frozen by their most serious ad-
herents, become intractable, and are applied for all
occasions. Brecht's theories were for the satisfaction

34

of critics and scholars, who were convinced that a process is authentic only when it is supported by a complex of fixed concepts. His theories were related to his intentions on the stage, but they were never fully evolved or fully realized. His intentions, moreover, were different from those of other leading theaters of his time: (1) he wanted to attack the bourgeois audience, which others made an all-out effort to please; (2) his theme was the cruelties and contradictions of man as a social creature, while other theaters were concerned with psychological problems; and (3) Brecht wanted a deliberate, conscious effect, while other theaters were interested in illusion or spontaneity.

It should be restated at once that the premise at the center of Brecht's work is that *people can change. Things could be different.* The epic theater, as he came to define and redefine it, asks for a removal of pity by the performers and audience, since pity is a response to that which cannot be changed: Brecht said "cling not to the wave breaking against your foot. As long as your foot stays in the water, on it new waves will break." Brecht wanted his audience to be actively interested students at a finely worked out epic classroom, where teachers of the same subject who had different points of view would argue out the lesson. The lesson is to be charged with entertainment, allegories, songs, impersonation, humor, clever, always-visible theatrical invention, and a unique kind of secrecy as a constant current during the whole event. It would be only for adults, because children are not concerned with such serious questions as choice. Adults largely determine the child's choice until he insists on making his own: at that point he is an adult too.

An initially useful inquiry into Brecht's theory of the actor is to compare his theory with that of Stanislavski. The Stanislavski system in its purest form is a road map guiding the actor to spontaneous expression of character through tasks which he sets up for himself in the form of internal actions. He learns how to involve himself personally in the character, until he can merge the character's inner life with its outer expression, and play out the event as though the audience were not present. When an actor breaks down his part (scores his role), he is constantly concerned with the stakes of his character, supporting the character's actions with the actor's motivations: the moment-to-moment reality becomes a circle of concentration which includes only the other characters.

Stanislavski was a director who directed other people's plays; in the main Brecht directed his own. What is radical in Brecht's requirement is that the actor as a private person be concerned with the matter of the entire play. In addition to his presence on the stage as the character in the given circumstances, he is sharing with the audience a response to the char-

36

acter's predicament. Each choice has to be made according to the logic of the playwright's intention, rather than exclusively with the character's. Moment to moment, the play is between actor and audience, as the actor's attitude changes about the character and his circumstances. The audience is the actor's partner as he plays the role of his character with the other characters. The actor does not have to wink, woo, or pander to win the audience's partnership; he begins with the assumption of partnership, and this assumption is the tacit understanding, the secret under the character façade.

Brechtian acting is analytical. That is: "I make a circle of involvement for myself as one would in a Stanislavski scene, but then I open it, in order to let the audience in." Three soldiers bribe Galy Gay with a box of cigars. He resists the offer. Then he capitulates. Brecht wanted the audience to see: (1) the ploys of the soldiers and Galy Gay's dilemma; and (2) the point at which this innocent can't say no. The four actors share the whole action (the bribe), each responsible for his own part of it: each actor's focus is the steps that make up the bribe. There is no interest in playing the details of each character which are irrelevant to the bribe. The particular choices each actor makes come out of exploring the forces which move the action toward Galy Gay's capitulation.

The usual mistake American actors make in trying to follow Brecht's suggestions lies in their interpretation of "detachment" or *Verfremdungseffekt*. Brecht first stated this idea of detachment as a theory when he defended Peter Lorre in his performance of *Man Is Man.* The critics said it was an unsatisfactory performance in that Lorre was not "involved" with the part of Galy Gay. Since he was not involved, they found him uninvolving. Brecht had admired Lorre's performance very much, and had steered him to the final result. So he came out inviting the critics and the public to enjoy Lorre's performance in a different way from that in which they ordinarily regarded the playing of a character. He began to discuss "detachment": An actor was to remain present in his impersonation of a character; he was not to merge with the character. It was to be more of a demonstration of the whole event, as in the example of the bribe, with each actor responsible for the actions of one particular character.

The whole notion of the V-effect is distorted in America because actors think "detachment" means "not caring." Quite the contrary. Whether or not Mother Courage bargains too long over Swiss Cheese's ransom, whether Grusha will take the infant aristocrat, these are actions with consequences of which the actor, like the audience, is aware. The V-effect is a means of presenting these events so that the audience can have an unsentimental view of them. It is anything but indifference. The difficulty is that our actors understand involvement only to be involvement

with the feelings of the character. If two people
nearly burn to death in a fire, their retelling of it, no
matter how detached, is different from that of two
people who are trying to arouse in themselves the
fantasized dread and peril of being in a burning
house. If what we see is merely a reproduction of
what exists, we will not understand it or our relationship to it.

Brecht constantly uses irony, humor, masks, songs,
and allegory to disturb our smugness and bend our
fixed logic, to focus a searchlight on the social
roles we play. He wanted to show that we live either
by values which we choose deliberately or, as most
often, by those at hand which we simply accept.
His themes are of man involved with society; man
suffering from a choice he may not himself have made;
man imprisoned in situations constructed by a system
he doesn't understand; man craving, choosing, pur-
suing, according to values set up by other men, dictated by ruthless economic and political forces which
bear the guise of simple expediency. The first requisite
for an actor approaching Brecht is to accept Brecht's
assumption that what takes place in the world is taking place within himself, and that the actor is connected to whatever takes place in the world. With this
understood, the actor should study the theories, appreciate how they came about, and then depart from
them: having understood this much, he will be faithful to Brecht's intentions.

39

Each actor is responsible to a particular character, but his attention is on the whole event. He must know the whole event in all its incongruities, seeing the chaos clearly. From that perspective we have a better view of the structures in which we live, these structures being arrangements we make to deal with chaos. Brecht asks us always to re-examine these arrangements.

It is important to know the Germany Brecht fled and returned to if one is to play Brecht, just as it is important to know the France Artaud was decomposing in, and the aristocratic Russia of Chekhov and Stanislavski. The Germany Brecht fled was the goose-step, the concentration camps, the songs, the massacres, executed in the name of the noblest virtues. It is not incidental that Brecht was writing in a Nazi world: he felt it directly, and he fled it.

But above all, Brecht wanted his theater to apply to the sensibility of the time, and would not have wanted it to be a museum theater. It is because of this that I believe Brecht must be performed in relation to what *is* vital, rather than what *was*. Many young people feel that *change* rather than *progress* is all one can see in terms of recorded history. A person is whom he pretends to be. While I put off taking any action for or against what I see, my life recedes before me. It passes. It passes. It passed. Brecht's works are intended to be a call to action—action as a form of choice, choice based on what I see. As Laing said in

The Politics of Experience:

If we are stripped of experience, we are stripped
of our deeds; and if our deeds are, so to speak,
taken out of our hands like toys from the hands
of children, we are bereft of humanity. We cannot be deceived. Men can and do destroy the
humanity of other men, and the condition of this
possibility is that we are interdependent. We are
not self-contained monads producing no effects
on each other except our reflections. We are
acted upon, changed for good or ill, by other
men; and we are agents who act upon others to
affect them in different ways. Each of us is the
other to the others.

IV

Notes on My Training

I started acting before I was in grade school. Recently, as a result of an article that appeared in the Des Moines paper about me and the Open Theater, I received a letter from the vice-principal of the high school I had gone to there. He said he was very proud that I had gone there and that he remembered me as a very good student. I remember that I almost failed every course I had; I couldn't concentrate on what anybody was talking about.

I'd been acting in grade school, but by the time I got to high school I began playing a lot of roles: high school repertory, Kaufman and Hart, that kind of thing, reproducing the stereotyped performances I had seen others do in previous semesters. After high school I stayed in Des Moines and went to Drake University, where I started to meet people in the theater. We worked on different contemporary plays, and then I started to do a lot of Shakespearean and Greek plays.

I went on to play Shakespeare at the college and began to study philosophy. I quit school after about three years and came to New York to begin studying with whoever it was that was recommended at the time; first it was at the Herbert Berghof Studio.

I did part-time office work, but I was incompetent, and got fired regularly. I never held a job very long—literally, days. I went to a temporary office service to rent myself out to them. I found ways of pretending that the equipment was not working—that it wasn't me, it was *it*. Finally, I gave up on offices and started working as a waiter. I had a very, very cheap apartment, lived on very little, and studied with everyone that was recommended, taking as many classes as I could afford.

STANISLAVSKI AND DOGMA

Each teacher I studied with taught the Stanislavski method in his own way, and each assured his devoted students that they would find "inner truth" *only* by subscribing to the specific method of that teacher. Generally, the teaching broke down into four kinds:

1. The principle of objectives, actions, and obstacles. This technique helps the actor draw from his character and circumstances (a) what his over-all objective in the play is, (b) what his dramatic action

must be in order to achieve this objective, and (c) what obstacles stand in his way. That is, he learns to find the dramatic collision which is at the center of every scene. Many actors, once they have mastered this vocabulary, respond to it with strength and clarity. But for others the terms remain obscure and their acting inarticulate.

2. Sensory attention and emotional recall. Here concentration and relaxation are emphasized. The text is disregarded and the actor is urged to show only what he is feeling at the moment. Improvisations that seem like psychotherapy are freely used. Again, some actors grow with the work, but others move into a state of despondency. My professional objection to this training is that it prepares the actor to play alone —he is completely locked out of any ensemble experience.

3. Logical analysis of the text. Every moment of the play is analyzed and scored in terms of the character, the situation, etc. And once the score is finished, it remains fixed, regardless of the actor you are playing with, the director, the audience, etc.

4. Inspiration. This teacher does not use direct criticism but "inspires" the actor by giving him a kind of spiritual blood transfusion.

Each teacher maintained that his technique was suitable for *all* material, contemporary and classic, and for every period and all styles. They assured us that the only problem was to understand the approach and practice it steadily and faithfully. My biggest disappointment was in the smugness of all my teachers; they accepted a predefined but unstated boundary. I've read all the Stanislavski books available in English and I can't separate his school-work from his theater-work, his theory from his practice.

INFLUENCES

The exercises of Nola Chilton, who was an early teacher of mine, opened an enormous area within a psychological approach. From Mira Rostiva I gained the subtlety of invisible intentions which crisscross each other all the time, making themselves visible. I have studied and been exposed to many other influences which I've repudiated or incorporated. There has been no single early influence which was greater than the dialogues I had with Judith Malina and Julian Beck. None of it involved exercises, acting, or specific techniques, because at the time I was a member of the Living Theater they did not inquire into stage behavior or ritual. But they were free of all the aspirations and assumptions of established theater. Most recently, the strongest influence on me has been the company of people with whom I've been working, and their ideas and their lives.

SUMMER STOCK

My first professional job was in a summer stock company in Pennsylvania, where I played the sidekick in *No Time for Sergeants.* I was excited beyond all measure. When I got there, we were told that each actor had to come up with the full "characterization" in one day and the production would be mounted in one week. After the morning break the director said he would have to replace me if I didn't come through with something funnier in the afternoon than I had in the morning. I came through with something he *found* funnier, on schedule. Performance was for summer vacationers; we counted laughs and adjusted nightly performances to the laughs. The company of actors was charged every night only by the laughs. We were not friendly with one another, and in one week of rehearsal and two of playing, we played out various roles of betrayal and regret. We tried to meet the audience on the dumbest common level.

After three weeks in stock I came back to New York. I made a point of telling everyone I met how exciting it was and what a success I had been. I tried to believe this. As long as it was in the past and no one was around to contradict the report, I could convince myself that it was a glamorous experience and that I was to be envied.

Once I officially dropped out of school, in addition to studying in the theater, I also continued studying philosophy. In this study I found a teacher named Dr. Julius Portnoy who was able to talk in the first person about each philosopher we studied. It was at this time that I began to think through the writings of the rationalists, the political philosophers, and the metaphysicians. I first experienced the joy of learning as opposed to the task of passing a course. I learned freely instead of trying to figure out what the teacher had in mind for me. I learned that it was all right to think of the inconceivable—a space without boundary. It was all right to imagine spheres where there were no answers but only speculation. Up to that point religion had always turned me off from the spiritual, and kept me from responding to all that's mysterious. Religion had been offered to me always in phony moral, bloodless, sexless fear packages.

About 1960 I went to the Living Theater. I got a part in a play they were doing, Paul Goodman's *From the Cave.* We rehearsed it for ten weeks, because everything kept going wrong technically—with the company, with the building; there was the threat of bankruptcy, and we kept being stopped, and the production kept being delayed. When the play opened it was a disappointment, but this put me into the repertory of the Living Theater. I played in *Many Loves* by William Carlos Williams, and eventually I got into *The Connection,* with a part for which I was ill-suited. After several months I realized I couldn't stand being in *The Connection* any more, and I went to a different theater where I played in De Ghelderode, a Yeats play, and an e. e. cummings play—mostly poetic theater. Then that closed, and I called up the

47

The Connection (1960): LEFT TO RIGHT, Joseph Chaikin, Gary Goodrow

Living Theater and said: "I have to go back to office work unless you give me work. I'll take anything." They said: "The only thing is *The Connection*. You can go back into that." So I went back into it.

We had made a European tour during my first period with the Living Theater and then we went to Europe again, this time adding a Brecht play, *In the Jungle of Cities*. After that, back to New York and a part in *Man Is Man*. This was the beginning of a radical change for me, and the end of a certain aspiration. Until the Brecht play I had been interested in a fancy career for myself as an actor, and I thought the opportunity to play this role would give me all the chance in the world to further this career.

I thought I was very happy: it was the beginning of stardom—Off-Broadway was just coming to be important—and I was playing a major role in a new play, with a company that was noticed and called interesting. I had a New York agent and a personal manager as well, and a lot of projects waiting. They would say: "We've got to get good reviews, and then we have to take them in such and such a way, and a movie will show up, and a this will show up . . ." We were trying to find out exactly how to label me— was I a young character or a character juvenile or an offhand young leading actor—exactly what was I?

But in doing the role every night, saying the lines, finding my own involvement with the play, I changed little by little. Like Galy Gay in the play, it came

Man Is Man (1962): LEFT TO RIGHT, Judith Malina, Joseph Chaikin

mostly from considering the lines of the play, night after night after night. And saying them. Studying them and saying them: there is a time when he turns to the audience and says, "Who am I? If they cut off my arm and my head, would the arm recognize the head?" It was particularly the responsibility of coming out to the audience and talking directly to them— something I had never had to do before—knowing that what I said to the audience I didn't believe, and then coming to believe what I was saying.

The other thing was the Becks. I had become involved with them originally simply as an actor to whom they had offered a part—not a very good part, but one that might lead to better ones. Behind this thinking was my ambition to be seen, my hope that I might really "get somewhere." But while I was with the Becks my idea of "somewhere" became very confused.

Politics was what undid it. I had resisted that aspect of their theater, because it had seemed ridiculous and unnecessary to me. The world didn't seem to me to be all that bad. I used to say to them again and again, "Are you a theater or are you a political movement? You can't be both." I was very determined to define my path, and it was their ambivalence about what they were doing that made my path appear clearer to me.

We had many conversations, and many fights. And what Judith and Julian were saying and doing, the lines of Galy Gay which I was saying every night to the audience, and the conversations I got into at that time began to have an impact on me. I started getting involved in political things, and getting involved in demonstrations, and getting arrested and going to jail. I was only there a couple of nights at a time, but it had a lasting effect on me. I began to feel that the political aspect of the Living Theater, which had looked so ridiculous, was very necessary. And the fact that it *was* ridiculous didn't make it any less necessary.

I began thinking, shortly after that, that I would like to know more about acting than I had access to through the classes I had been going to, or through the Living Theater. At that time the Living Theater was not really interested in acting at all, and hardly explored the actor's own powers or the ensemble experience. The constant state of emergency at the Living Theater prevented that. So I began working with writers and actors from Nola Chilton's class after she had gone to Israel—people who wanted to continue working together even though she was gone. When the Living Theater went to Europe in 1963, I did not.

Our new group began meeting once a week, and then twice a week. Our first problem arose when the actors wanted to continue exactly as Nola had done when she worked with them, and I wanted us to try

JOSEPH CHAIKIN

other things. And again there was a certain dogmatic
hurdle: *this* is the way, and another way is not the
way. It was a very transient situation, where people
came and went. We took a long time to see if we could
trust each other, and given the way we defined the
question, we found we couldn't. There were a number
of experiments within a classroom and workshop situation: some of them were attempts to relate and understand certain Brechtian ideas, some of them were
political, some were ideas I had had for a long time
and wanted to develop with other people, and a
great many of them were simply to take away the
wall, the boundary—that limit we felt through our
training. We began by doing things like tying up our
hands and legs and trying to perform a task with
another actor, trying to find some other way than
using naturalistic mannerisms.

The internal questions were "What direction
should we take?" and "Do you think we can get along
with each other?" At this point there were two schools
of thought, one that felt we should be basically a communal group doing theater, and the other that felt we
should be a group of theater professionals. These
questions occurred again and again. And then we said,
Well, what name should we give ourselves? And we
thought of all kinds of names, including the Genesis,
the Spiral, and the Open Theater. I liked the Open
Theater because it was an unconfining name, it im-

53

plied a susceptibility to continue to change. The name would serve to remind us of that early commitment to stay in process, and we called ourselves that.

1964

Very early in our meetings, even before we started calling ourselves the Open Theater, we were a formless group. The initial form came about as a result of the people who originally made up the group. Lee Worley, Peter Feldman, and Meg Terry were there from the start. Their temperaments and talents largely shaped the first period of the Open Theater. After meeting for two or three or four months, Jean-Claude van Itallie was brought to a workshop by Gordon Rogoff. His role in the early stages, and our collaboration from that point, beginning with short scenes through *America Hurrah* and *The Serpent*, had a great deal to do with all that followed.

Julian Beck said that an actor has to be like Columbus: he has to go out and discover something, and come back and report on what he discovers. Voyages have to be taken, but there has to be a place to come back to, and this place has to be different from the established theater. It is not likely to be a business place.

One has to be able to imagine and feel an alternative realm of behavior in order to play it. The spectator will feel that what is true on the stage is what most represents himself—that realm which he most identifies with as his "real life" and perhaps that one which he most inhabits. But at the same time, the realm which is played recommends a "reality" which he may adopt.

Everything we do changes us a little, even when we purport to be indifferent to what we've done. And what we witness, we also do.

V

Notes to the Actors—1965

When you take a job in the current business theater, you must become the size and shape of that job. At the Open Theater we have the feeling that this is not enough. It is not possible to make discoveries under the pressure to please, to gain audiences, and to make money. It is necessary to close off the impulse to "make it" in order to open oneself.

One of the good things is that we're willing to fail; it helps us go beyond the safe limits and become adventurers. This quality comes to a group only when each person hās gone through suspicion and now trusts the other. It is never possible among actors who are together only for a single show. The creative impulse can't grow in a climate of competition (like auditions) where it is necessary to prove one's value. Nor can acting classes whose purpose is to groom the actor for hiring take the time or risk to experiment with what the *teacher* doesn't know. But working with the "don't knows" is perhaps more important than teaching the "knows."

The assumption. It would be good for certain boundaries, tacit as well as defined, to be broken. It would be good to have a tossing up of values and experiment with the comedy of sincerity, breaking down the structure that we work within, like a person whose habits in living have him impaled in patterns of acting which anchor him. It would be good to change the relationships which we are frozen in: Theater, audiences', directors', and actors' relationships. Other kinds of recognition scenes must be played out.

WINTER 1965

The organization of the Open Theater has changed its face already so many times that it is hard to know what is referred to as the Open Theater. The structure and emphasis is always changing: I have no idea what will happen in the future. But even if we were to melt away now, I think we would have already unfixed what previously seemed almost immovable in our work. Somehow, our minds are stirred. The movies have come such a distance in understanding their art and broadening it, while the stage remains stuck in the thirties. But everything—including impenetrable audiences—is changing, and the old work is no longer enough. If Stanislavski were alive, would he be working in the same way, or would he be exploring? The obvious answer is the challenge of his example, which our theater rarely meets.

Only some of our work and thought is in social terms. Much of the work is abstract and nonliteral. When we begin on a new form or idea, we have no way of knowing if it will result in anything visible or lend any clarity. Often it doesn't.

The Actor's Study

It's hardly enough for an actor to expose himself to the theater and theater schools. An actor must involve himself with different ways of perceiving besides his own. An introduction to being able to put himself in someone else's shoes is often clearest through the senses.

There are many opportunities for an actor to make contact with the blind and deaf through volunteer work.

An actor should visit and inspect patients in hospitals, and he should go to night courts, Buddhist services, A. A. meetings, draft boards, ghettoes, Bowery flophouses, and public bars of different kinds; otherwise he has only a partial understanding of the dimension of his study.

An actor must also have exposure to different

group-identity situations such as prisons and crim-
inal organizations. Without this kind of inquiry into
other forms of living, the actor is simply working off
the top of society's crust where very special advantages are on display.

THE ENSEMBLE

Technically speaking, I understand ensemble work
to have two principles. The first is empathy: one
actor, instead of necessarily competing with another,
instead of trying to take attention away from him,
would instead support the other. (Acting always has
to do with attention, and with where the attention is.)
There comes a point where you no longer know
exactly which actor is in support and which actor
initiated the action; they are simply together.

The other has to do with rhythm, with dynamics,
and with a kind of sensitivity which could be rhyth-
mically self-expressed. For example, there is a kind of
inner rhythm going on all the time in any single
person. If you would let the body go with the rhythm,
you would discover that there is a pattern and a
dynamic and an intensity that would change as experience changed during the day, a quality which,
if you knew somebody else well, you could say is the
theme of that person's rhythm. This is the rhythm
in a room and it affects the room and it charges the
room and it charges the people. Sometimes there is a
kind of rhythmic battle that goes on between people

when they might be quite in accord on what they're talking about. There is a kind of clash of certain rhythms, and sometimes rhythms and inner dynamics get together and sometimes they counterpoint. This work has been the second main concern in building the ensemble.

THE ENSEMBLE AND RECOGNITION

John has a thought (an impulse, an inspiration, an idea). He finds a *way* (approach) to convey this to Jane. If she doesn't recognize it, he must look for another way. If she doesn't recognize it, no matter how many ways he finds to demonstrate it, they cannot go further in their collaboration on it. If Jane does recognize John's thought, they can collaborate.

Next they look for a *way* to project this idea to a spectator. They address themselves to the spectator, who would be potentially capable of recognizing it, if John and Jane find the *way*. John and Jane together now try to do with the spectator what John did with Jane.

The process of collaboration is the work of an ensemble.

That which the collaborators choose is the act. Their approach is contained in the act. The act is to cause recognition for the spectator. The process is the mysterious involvement of the collaborators, which leads to choosing the act. The deliberate means which they use, such as exercises, discussion, field work, etc.,

60

are the conscious elements within the process. The technique is the disciplines and the rules on how to use the conscious elements.

If the actors think that the audience cannot potentially recognize what they are doing, they cannot find an approach which would be recognizable.

The Serpent—*1968*

Within the theater it is often believed that except for the concerns of the particular character an actor is playing, the less he knows about the implications of a work, the better. In a work like *The Serpent* the actor must understand as much as can be understood. Here the ideas in the piece are as important to the actor's understanding as are his individual character motivations. Since the strength of the production rests on the power of the ensemble of actors, the ensemble must address itself to the questions and images which make up *The Serpent*. The most hazardous and rewarding problem in a group effort such as this one is to find communal points of reference.

Because the main part of the piece is taken from a narrative, the story of Genesis in the Bible, it is important that the group of actors first look for images which come close to their own early pictures of these stories. The more faithful their images are to their own garden-in-the-mind, to Adam and Eve, etc., the closer they will be to attaining a place of recognition.

While working on the garden sequence of *The Serpent*, the premise was that everyone had his garden-in-the-mind, this place that the world isn't, this utopia—where creatures are themselves. The creatures who live in this garden are compatible with each other. We went first of all toward breaking, destroying the false Garden pictures: the illustrated biblical ones, the modern Hollywood ones, those from *House and Garden*—all the commercials (riding and Marlboros). But we had to find a place where we could play out this garden. A place to meet, after getting rid of the false notions.

A theater event should burn into time as a movement cuts into space. Time is experienced only in terms of rhythm. To "recognize" is to awaken to what is taking place.

An authentic image came; somebody got on the stage and introduced it. The stage is totally empty. The action is to appreciate its emptiness as much as possible, so as not to see the things that could be there but to imagine it as empty. And to then project on it the image of your garden. One actor will get up and do his garden and if another actor is sensitive to it, he will join him so that they make a little world.

62

The Serpent (1968): LEFT TO RIGHT, Peter Maloney, Ralph Lee, Ray Barry, Ron Faber

A third actor may or may not join, depending on whether this garden does or does not signal anybody else, and whether or not it gives them something they can identify with and understand. Then it's over and someone else tries it. Soon somebody will start a world with its own logic, its own rules, and its own sense. Then we have the garden.

When questions are alive to a company of actors, there is in any of them a dangerous point when discussion must stop and the questions must be brought to the stage in terms of improvising actions. There are two main values in working on a piece in this way, collaboratively. One is the affirming discovery of finding deep common references. It takes time to reach these; the cliché references often come out first. And the second value is the discovery of the astonishing power there is in the performance of an actor who is actually playing out an image which he himself introduced.

Don't sing your voice. Find and sing the song. It sounds easy. But it's that kind of ease which usually follows many false starts, like a phrase of music which just came to the composer after struggling with the whole symphony. Discoveries are usually made after one exhausts trying through the planned means.

The most articulate performances are always those which have been pared away. All that's nonessential, all that's accessory, all that's indulgent, all that's outside the center has been dropped, and what remains is a spare language of tasks which speak of life and nature.

The things which you know very well you can leave out and they will be there. The things which you don't know well you will probably overdescribe.

—HEMINGWAY

The basic starting point for the actor is that his body is sensitive to the immediate landscape where he is performing. The full attention of the mind and body should be awake in that very space and in that very time (not an idea of time) and with the very people who are also in that time and space.

The industrial mainstream of society is always a pressure to make of us "achievers," to make of us "goods." Many of our appetites are developed by the industrial society, and most of our models are not freely picked by us.

We are trained and conditioned to be "present" only in relation to the goal. When I go from my house to the grocer, I'm not present. Once I arrive at the grocer, I'm not present until I'm back at the house. Going from point A to B we are in a kind of nonlife, and from B to C the same. This is one of our earliest lessons . . . to be in relation to the goal. This teaches us to live in absent time.

65

The actor must compose the rules he goes by. The technique of the actor is an inner discipline. The first step in preparation for an actor, and very often the longest step, is for the actor to find in himself one clear place. Quite often the actor mistakenly assumes that his preparation should consist of filling himself with broad emotional experiences. Instead, the actor must find an empty place where the living current moves through him uninformed. A clear place. Let's say the place from where the breath is drawn . . . not the breath . . . but from where the inhalation starts. An actor who is fully emotionally prepared is overwhelming his internal life, is filling the cleared space, and all this functions against discovery.

There are streams of human experiences which are deep and constant, moving through us on a level below sound. As we become occupied with our own noises, we're unable to be in the stream. The more an actor boasts of his feeling as he feels it, the farther he is from the current.

First, the actor must be present in his body, present in his voice. Second, the body must be awake—all of it, the parts and the whole—and it must be sensitive to reaction through imaginary and immediate stimuli. The voice must be alive and exist in its life within the space in the room. It must be sensitive to stimuli in the room from the mind and deep in the body. The voice originates inside the body and comes to exist in the room. The senses must be awake to what's happening and to what's being created, transforming the space, always able to return to the quiet inner starting point. That quiet inner place is always there, whether you are in contact with it or not.

We must be able to go somewhere else—where, we don't know. The danger here is that we will get lost.

In *The Serpent* the Garden of Eden begins with a cue—one, two, three, ready—a number of people are on the frame of what we make the stage, responding to a technical cue, performing movements that have been carefully chosen over a thousand others. None of us believe there is or ever was a real Garden of Eden, but it lives in the mind as certainly as memory. For us it's a gathering of creatures who breathe together and are vibrantly alive and become an organized world.

The danger is that we will get lost. Plan on it: count on it.

V I

Notes on Actor and Salesman

Does it require deep intuition to comprehend that man's ideas, views and conceptions, in one word, man's consciousness, changes with every change in the condition of his material existence, in his social relations and in his social life?

—Marx and Engels, 1848

One thing I think about a lot, and so far without any answers, is the question of whether you can do something in one part of your life that you couldn't do in another. In the theater, for example, can you—not having fulfilled thirty things you wish you had in your life—can you realize them in the theater? My feeling is that you can. On the stage you do not have to regard situations with the same degree of finality as in life. There it is possible to create and repudiate circumstances of your life.

68

JOSEPH CHAIKIN

THE PERFORMANCE OF PERSON

If there's a party I want to go to, I try to find out
what it takes to get invited. It's the host who determines the requirements. (Just as to own a coat and
tie might be the requirement for one party, other
parties have just as specific eligibility standards.)
Once I find what the requirements are, I start to
gather them for myself. Once I meet the requirements, I demonstrate or even flaunt my eligibility to
the host. Then I wait for an invitation.

The "acting" etiquette which we subscribe to or
renounce is recommended to us through movie stars
and heads of state such as presidents, first ladies,
mayors, etc.

Johnny Carson doesn't appear to be acting while
he hosts a talk show on TV, but he is. He is performing himself, and in so doing he *recommends* a way
to perform. As you attend his party, you are at once
being trained for eligibility. Attending a party is
itself an apprenticeship toward becoming a host. At
this party you also learn to perform yourself and
to stylize yourself. This form of stylization is *recommended* as a way of making oneself visible, recognizable, and comprehensible to another.

Social man is the man in relation to the party, the
person as actor. Public figures, such as politicians and
priests, are acting in their public role. Choosing
clothes is picking costume. Actors, while they are
acting, are recommending. Actors, through their

acting, are validating a definition of identity and rendering other definitions invalid. Recommending a way to perform oneself is working to sell a mode of being.

Helen Hayes appears at Christmastime with a commercial for polio victims or the Red Cross. As she finishes the commercial, she puts down her script and looks steadily at us. We know that she is just a person, like every complicated person, and yet, for the moment, we know that is not *all* she is. She is embodying a cultural icon, the presentation of a good person. She presents a form of women-kindness.

Richard Nixon in a television speech reads from a paper in a formal mode. Later he puts the paper down and says, "Now, friends, I'm not going to talk to you formally. Instead I want to talk to you directly." In that one speech he formalized two different presentations. Each one was acted with a different disguise of "sincerity."

Another tone of presentation comes from the pulpit. As a preacher talks, whatever the information he is giving—how to live, what the afterlife is like, what you should think—at the same time he is establishing (recommending) himself as a *good* person. The American psychiatrist Harry Stack Sullivan classified different attitudes a person has toward his actions. One says, "I do this action from the 'good me,' the me I respect and encourage"; another says, "I do this other action out of the 'bad me,' the me which always misbehaves and which one day I hope to have sovereignty over"; the third says, "this is 'not me'—I do it though I have no claim to it, I don't know where it comes from, it was an expression of something which is not an authentic part of me." The professional minister, no matter what he is saying, is expressing something from the "good me" to the "good you," for your benefit and with the aim of reinforcing the "good us." It is the same with the cultural icon which Helen Hayes is using: *I am speaking for your benefit, I am revealing my goodness for your benefit—for mine too, perhaps—and I ask you to appreciate it and accept it for your benefit.*

If you don't appreciate it, if you don't accept it, then you are probably misguided, but more dangerous, you are rejecting the "good me." If you reject the me that I respect and encourage, then all I am left with is the "bad me," and the "not me." I need to protect my personal "setup" if I'm to continue. I might even have to go so far as to bomb you, to blast you, to kill you, *for your benefit,* and to preserve the "good us."

John Wayne, who is part of the current mythology of characters, said recently on TV: "There is not one moment of my life that I am not proud to be an American. America first!" There are now two John Waynes—a public political personality as well as John Wayne the icon actor. As the latter, John Wayne is only John Wayne: it doesn't really matter what movie he is in. It is all a masquerade, where we all know the person behind the mask and the person who is masked doesn't even try to be anybody else. It is John Wayne, this guy, this hero, my father's buddy. He can protect the wife and kids, they have nothing to worry about should a burglar come in the middle of the night. He is patriotic, he would as soon fight for his country as for his wife and kids in the middle of the night. We are to fear his strength and to emulate it.

What is important are the gestures, the presentation of the mask. The act is incidental; to inhabit the act is in fact unnecessary; it is the acting of it that counts. It is on the basis of the acting that another person says *This is a man* or *This is a good person*.

Then there are people who indicate how we can suffer beautifully: if you can suffer the way Ingrid Bergman suffers, then it is not all that bad to suffer.

These actors who become icon-star-favorites have a lot to do with our lives. Here are two people, and they start seeing each other and at a certain point something deeper starts to happen, a kind of enchantment, a more urgent attachment than when they first met. The time comes when one of them wants to declare that he loves the other: it is a statement of commitment that he finally feels necessary to declare to the other person, and no longer hold inside himself. As he says, "I love you," all the movies he has ever seen come rushing between him and the other person. Immediately he starts to compare what is happening to him with a filmed romance. He experiences the hollowness of the words—there seems to be an absence and in fact, as he says, "I love you," he sneakily feels he lies.

These two people are standing together, holding hands, with Shelley Winters and Gary Cooper right between them, and the experience they are having doesn't resemble the thing that happened when Shelley Winters said it to Gary Cooper at all. They are somewhere between their own unique experience and that particular stereotyped thing, and they just bounce back and forth, trying in some way to find a balance for themselves. It is frustrating because they can't really do it, and they can't keep from trying to do it.

How does something become valid? If we can make our experience resemble the one in the movies, or if we can deceive ourselves into saying it resembles it, then the movies validate our real experience. We are intimidated by the fictional experience, not just because theirs is big and ours is little, but because theirs is authentic, ours is warped, out of gear, unintended.

The more confused and chaotic the era is, the more these icon personalities are taken on as models. With the icons each one of us has his pick of one of his own age, sex, and cultural level. They serve an extremely important function and sustain all kinds of misperceptions, all of which help keep things going as they are.

Take dry-cleaning establishments. Here is one that has lollipops and Tootsie Rolls in a little bowl. That's a nice touch, and who doesn't enjoy a Tootsie Roll? You come in there and somehow that dry-cleaning store has it over another one that doesn't have Tootsie Rolls, even if the other is identical. Then there is another dry cleaner I know of that sometimes sews on a button for you. Free. That is a very big feature, because you don't want to go to the trouble of "how much was the button?" and so on. The one that has the Tootsie Rolls doesn't do buttons. Then there is a third one: this one has friendliness. It can be friendly to you, and your child, and your aunt, and ask how you are. This one does the most business of the three, but each of them is doing its particular service to get more business and more customers. As for the one that is being friendly, the more expensive stores have a much more deferential manner than the cheaper ones; one easily buys respect and a kind of gentleness. The cleaning store that asks about my health charges more than the other two. Recently, I went to get two pairs of pants tapered at the legs. I said, "How much will they cost?" The guy said, "One leg, two legs, three legs, four—that's four dollars." He didn't have to count legs: everybody knows how many legs there are in two pairs of pants. It's part of the game.

The most successful aspect of persuasion is that people are made to aspire to things they don't even want. How do you get to want these things?

A person's whole character and manner finally turns into a commercial for one thing or another. The

74

question I have to ask myself, as an actor, is no
longer merely "What do I want and how do I go after
it?" but *"What makes me want what I want?"*

The University of TV. TV programs become the
recommended personal fantasies to be shared by all,
and TV is successful because many millions of people
at once are given a very similar repertoire of fantasy
and experience. It becomes one of the most effective
ways of manipulating the imagination through establishing a common premise and promoting a uniform
inner life. The talk shows become a functional way
of giving a code of behavior to the viewers, while the
game shows give signals as to what the correct associations are, all played out in a form of American
charm. This façade is essential in the same way a
stylized cordiality is necessary between enemy leaders
when they meet together. As in any contest which
gives the illusion of only one winner, we are potentially each other's enemy. What is central to the
marathon is respect for it. Once a person withdraws
respect, he cannot enter into the "promising" class.
But once he has been admitted to the "promising"
class, he has already learned the correct associations
and how to apply them. As long as he applies them,
his deeper responses have no effect on anything outside his private dreams. He has done his part to sustain the unbroken circle.

The danger in breaking the circle is that then we
would see that there are really other goals and other
places to inhabit.

VII

Notes on Acting in Terminal

Among others, a theme which was dropped from *Terminal* was a series of descriptions of the "death place." What was its society? Were there rules? Is it like the living world? What is the interrelationship of the dead with each other? Is there a hierarchy? What are the rewards and punishments? Do the dead have bodies? If not, then what contains that individual dead one?

Is there a different death place for each individual dead?

In which death place are you?

1. I'm in the death where I can say what I see but not what I think.
2. I'm in the death of forgetfulness where I've forgotten all I knew or dreamt. I remember only one thing and it's all I ever think or remember.
3. I'm in the death where I live together with a species of jackasses and they speak together in

their language, which I don't understand, and they can't understand me when I speak in my language.

4. I'm in the death of disguises. Where I am, nothing is what it is and no one is who he is. Everything is disguised.

5. I'm in the death of hope. I hope and wish, yet nothing moves or changes. Everything is frozen. Still, I have the hope I had when I was alive. Here I am consumed by hope, even though I see that nothing moves or can move by my hoping for it.

6. I'm in the death of crowds. There are multitudes here where I am, and they are each one myself. We are surrounded by us. There is not one other here beside me, yet there are multitudes.*

7. I'm in the death of constant regret for every action I took and each action I didn't take while I was alive. I'm consumed with regret.

8. I'm in the death of rage for every action I took, and each action I didn't take. I'm consumed with rage.

9. While I lived I thought, "How can I live knowing I will die? How can I love knowing it will end?" Here nothing ends. That is the death I'm in.

We tried many forms of description for the "death place"—the dead sitting upright on hard-backed chairs, the dead hanging by the tails of animallike creatures, and many very abstract physical positions.

* This section (number 6) was the only one actually used in *Terminal*.

As we worked on the "death place," it seemed that it would take as much time to define it as it would to work out the rest of the piece. Also, each attempt seemed far richer as an idea than when actually played out.

We began with an idea of trying to confront the dread of dying. The ward starts us off with a look at life as a process of death where death is tucked away under an elaborate conspiracy in which even the conspirators are deceived. This conspiracy to make a person distracted from his own inevitable death helps to get him so intensely involved with those distractions and values of the world, that one could say: "My mission is to make as much money as I can, my mission is to have seven cars like someone I once knew, my mission is to achieve in those terms set down by others." The conspirators are deceived and participate in the conspiracy which they perpetrate. By doing this, they feel that they are honest: they have accepted the deception.

TO THE ACTORS PREPARING
TERMINAL — SEPTEMBER 1969

My experience with Jerzy Grotowski this summer was very valuable—it gave me a lot of nourishment, many things to consider, and many things to question. He uses some terms which seem specific and clear to me. They harness ideas that otherwise are hard to articulate.

I by no means take his approach as my own, and I'm convinced that the approach of the Polish Lab Theatre would not benefit us, but the kind of challenge he forces you to take and his severe criteria for self-criticism has had a significant effect on me, and you may notice that in part of this talk.

Plans change and go in directions which you don't necessarily expect, but most of the points in this talk relate to this group and this piece that we are now working on.

I think it's very possible, after this piece, that some of you who are acting in this work will want to direct and initiate work on your own, and that will be very good—but after this project I'll be working in a concentrated way and on a smaller scale. Even though there are many difficulties in this kind of thing, I love this work; but it's very, very hard, and the next chapter of projects which I initiate will be smaller in scale.

I intend to be much tougher in terms of feedback and criticism than I have been. Somehow there's a kind of invisible bribe that to say something critical is "unfriendly." There's no friendliness without criticism. It's difficult for me to be critical in a certain way, but I'm committing myself to that.

As I give criticism, you of course must always know that it's my point of view, not the "truth." You can reject or accept it on that basis.

We must find the conditions that make it possible to grow, because so many things in the world conspire against growth, and even if conditions were ideal, we'd still find there are seasons of growing and seasons of staying. An atmosphere which is creative and concentrated is like an incubation chamber, and it's dangerous to confuse that creative atmosphere with simply a friendly one.

Any moment one is alive is potentially a possibility to grow. We are a large group and we are not all in the same process at the same time, so if one is unable to move at a given time he shouldn't be in the way of the next.

Discipline is essential to anything ambitious, but the ultimate discipline is internal. If someone tells you to go stand on your head for half an hour and then do sixty somersaults, that may have value as an example of a process of discipline, but it isn't the real thing: it's just doing what someone tells you to do. You have to find the discipline necessary for yourself —a voluntary discipline. Because of the way things are in this country, we often act out of a dictate that has nothing to do with ourselves. We mustn't take that into our work, for, if we do, we won't be able to recognize our own impulses; what's essential, then, is a vigorous voluntary discipline.

Theaters like those in Poland and Holstebro in Denmark go in for a very heavy external discipline in order to call on a corresponding inner control. Sometimes people take the physical discipline to be an end in itself, but it's all meant to be taken together.

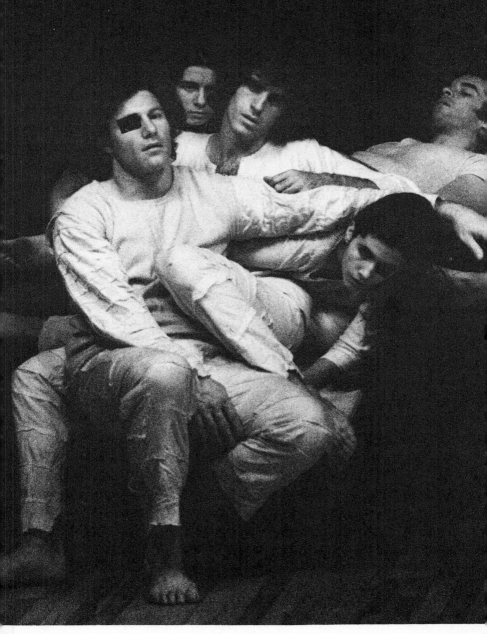

Terminal (1971): LEFT TO RIGHT, Raymond Barry, Tina Shepard, Paul Zimet, Joanne Schmidman, Henry Smith

Some of you are very prepared for discipline and others are lazy. Some of you are more gifted and others less. My being able to say this is part of the tyranny of my position as the director, because there's a good chance that we wouldn't agree on who is which. But it's my position that entitles me to make choices based on my assessment. On this score there has never been equality in any creative situation—dance, voice, painting, writing, theater.

No one in this group is uninspired and no one is untrained, but all in different degrees and with different orientation—and here we are together.

During working hours there must be no couples or best friends—only before and after.

What's important in our work is that we can in some way discover and later articulate our crisis . . . that crisis which pertains to us. But what kind of crisis is it? That of earning a living, the frustrations of interpersonal relations, the male and female questions, or what? Beyond that is a crisis that's very deep and has to do with the first assumption of "who I am," not as an ego, but as life with an illusory ego, and as a capacity so great that even as our personalities become shaped by this pernicious society which really believes it's better to get airports working more efficiently than to keep Harlem Hospital open— where our ideal course is clearly charted in front of us and the utopia we are intended to aim toward is a kind of Disneyland—we can see something of the life we are inside, the life we are being shaped to be.

This life can be imagined and dreamt and sometimes experienced. If all we stay with are our hangups, and we define ourselves completely in relation to them and get all excited in our work when we find an expressive release for them, we haven't got very far.

(Incidentally, each of you should see a Disney movie production within the next month, because that's really where they want us to think it's at.)

We are driven—like oxen—to think and understand and perceive as we do. When you stand on the top of a hill and a cloud covers the sun, it feels as though possibility has eclipsed. Then when the sun comes back, possibility opens again. In some part we're controlled by outer weather.

What's less clear is the way we're controlled and driven by the givens of society. It's a highly unenlightened society, but still it's our own—our own environment.

We are made to cherish things we don't even care about, and to give up things we fundamentally cherish. Very often we don't really *need* what we feel we *lack*.

I harp on this phenomenon because we're still living in post-Freudian times when it's held that all the controls are from within and that they come to exist because of psychic conditioning.

After each year of work I think, "what a bunch of crap that was last year." My feeling at a given time is "now is the only possibility." Some people I come across, for example, say they loved or hated *The Serpent*, or *The Clown Play*, or *America Hurrah*, or *The Body-Eating*—either way I feel limited by their response. One flatters and the other hurts, but both make me feel limited.

At those times when I feel flattered, I swell up with self-boasting and I feel a puffed-up chest and head. I know I would rather be able to forget myself. When I forget myself, I feel I am what happens in the room I'm in—not something else. But the feeling of being inflated or hurt should be dismissed. I think the best way of hearing criticism is to do it in three stages. The first stage is to accept the criticism unconditionally, thereby leaving yourself open to full consideration of it. The second stage is to regard the criticism skeptically and consider if it is in line with your direction. The third stage is to completely dismiss it from consciousness, having already assimilated whatever is valid into your efforts. My own rejection of all that comes before now comes in part from my general skepticism about theater, and in part from the fact that I know that all we've done is scratch the surface, and only the first layer of the surface.

Unless we wish to address ourselves fully to the material and to move with it and accept the frustrations involved, nothing else can follow. How serious an actor is has to do with the degree to which he takes his acting as something which is working through his deepest self. How skillful he is depends on how developed his resources are, so that he can articulate his experience as a shared living reality.

What we know of another person comes through the voice and the body. If the voice of the actor is limited to the reporting of the sounds we use for conversation and the body is fastened to the repertoire of sitting, standing, and fending off, there is the same potential for articulation as there is over coffee and a danish.

I don't mean simply that physical and vocal range is important, but that a total sensitivity is—so that the jaw or the torso can accomplish as clear a description as the full use of the body. The first thing we always have to do is unlock the body and the voice from the ruts into which they fall in everyday life, and move from there. My criticism will be in terms of where things seem to be locked. The balance we have to keep is how to discourage ourselves from going in directions which are noncreative, indulgent, and in imitation of constrictive social attitudes, while at the same time leaving ourselves open and available to the tides which are full of life and energy, informed from a vast and infinite place which enlarges. The first requires blocking, the second entails being out of the way; this is a hard balance to maintain.

This piece on death—why? Because death is connected to the greatest terror and the greatest dread. This zone of feeling relating to death is in the zone of the deepest feelings and mystery. Dying is the subject because it's the greatest taboo (both personal and societal), because it's a subject we all have to cope with and answer to, including each spectator, and because we're all in the same place in relation to it. If you think you have no relation to your own impermanence if you think it's antilife to work in that area, then you're involved in self-mystification. If the subject of dying still seems to you beside the point, you should think seriously if you want to be in the piece at all, because we can only start from our interest and the direction the piece will eventually take will be what we work out together. If you find death too depressing to think about, then you are on the wrong train; and you will have to face that and then go through it and beyond it.

In regard to this piece, if you're not interested in it, don't be in it. As we work on this piece, it's going to be rough and time is short, and *this* is the time to assess your interest. A cooperation that comes about through mutual interest is essential.

I rarely give praise in the workshop. I always feel that most of you are developed enough to know as you work whether or not you are working from your own nature. Even though we must sometimes be supported and encouraged, praise is beside the point. Even self-praise.

A very complicated and difficult problem is the relation of work to life and to this ensemble as a group, and our relationship to each other within it. There are many ways of settling this question and different people and groups find different solutions. None of the solutions are foolproof, from what I can see. We have more or less said we are a task group: we work through problems in order to perform a work as a group. We don't meet specifically to confront one another in our lives—our attitudes and interrelationships. We've said individually, more or less: "I have a private life of activities and friends who may overlap with the Open Theater, but it is also separate." Much of the work we do requires taking a lot of risk. The experiences we've had together have built up a lot of trust, which makes taking risks more possible. At the same time, nobody's able to shut out completely the pettiness we indulge in with our landlords when we come here. When we start work here, we aren't able to rise above envy and anxiety in outside personal relationships. We are not immune to flattery.

Our own settlement of work to life and ensemble to community undoubtedly will change, but because we can't close the door on pettiness in ourselves, we must become aware of it in order to subordinate it to the task at hand. This will always be a live problem, as it is now, and as it has been in all serious groups.

We have to be informed by life and experience, not simply to inform. We can't be informed if we already know what the character of an experience is to be. We must be in touch with our continual astonishment and bewilderment, or we can at best only protect ourselves from small hurts while going through life like a tech rehearsal.

The model to have while working on this piece is that of a physician. He gets all upset when he studies diseases. He thinks he has all the symptoms. He goes into a ward and sees people who are helpless and he wants to cry. The first person he sees die makes him vomit. The patient whom he's unable to do anything for throws him into a rage of frustration. Finally, he moves through and beyond these feelings and starts to perform as a doctor and live his life and do his work. If we stop where we are depressed, or even where we're satisfied with simply expressing our depression, we're dilettantes. If an area of life, like death, is too frightening and morbid to conceive of, we're stuck with the little pettinesses which we come up against at the rate of four every half-hour as the main matter of life. We have to conceive fully of the themes in the piece. We have enough problems in putting it together, selecting and rehearsing to last us beyond the weeks we're working on it. The matter of fully conceiving is a purely individual one. Since I was a child, I've had a defective heart, and perhaps because of my experiences with my heart condition, the reality of death is closer for me, but you don't have to put yourself through such an experience to conceive it. What do you have to do?

Finding a vocabulary about dying is what we have to do. It's not an easy thing, but not doing it will limit us. There's hardly anything more personal. So how do we find a vocabulary that can be made up of signs which are held in common meaning? During

The Serpent we were obsessed with the effect of the
Genesis story on ourselves, and with our attitudes
regarding guilt and the wrathful God. Now we shall
become obsessed with dying, but not in a sentimental
way.

The sentimental attitudes have to do with happiness
and fulfillment. This fallacy of happiness is written
into the Declaration of Independence, dramatically
ending it with "the pursuit of happiness" as a fundamental right. Happiness is the goal. Happiness is a
constant pleasure. Pleasure is a mild but consuming
delight, such as the first taste of a frozen custard, so
the idea of happiness is a constant little peak, and
then we're back to Disneyland and the American
myth. It's a certain kind of mystification which includes a warm glow. It's an entirely nostalgic and
log-cabin mysticism, so that someone who blows out
all but one of his birthday candles is left with a feeling
of dismay. It's a small thrill not coming from the
groin and belly but from the neck: the oceanic principle in a home pool. We're taught to strive for this
state above all others, and the striving feeds directly
into the "moronization" of us Americans. I think I've
experienced the warm glow in a totally consuming
way on those occasions when I've been stoned on
heroin. Coming off heroin is almost the opposite state
and repudiates all that preceded it, but I said to myself
that it doesn't matter, because for an hour and a half
everything *did* make sense and there *was* harmony
and a warm glow. It's the end of the Cinderella story,

with lovely Cinderella triumphing over her ugly sisters and being rescued finally by the rich prince. It's enchantment.

Susan Yankowitz was the writer of *Terminal*.

FINAL OUTLINE OF TERMINAL

The Calling Up of the Dead
The Pregnant Dying
    Taking in and Eliminating
    Motion
    Breathing
    Biological Rites
The Dance on the Graves of the Dead
Embalming as Required by Law
The Interview
THE DEAD COME THROUGH
    Marie Laveau and the Soldier
Cosmetics
The Runner Who Never Gets Started
THE DEAD COME THROUGH
    The Responsible One
The Dying Pray
The Initiation
The Witnesses
THE DEAD COME THROUGH
    The Executed Man and the Song
Embalming as Required by Law
The Dying Imagine Their Judgment
"The Judgment of Your Life Is Your Life"

VIII

Notes on Myself

When I was in grade school, my family was very poor. During that time, I was sick with rheumatic fever, and stayed home a lot, because they couldn't afford to send me to the hospital. After recovery, which took almost two years, I was wheeled around in a baby carriage, even though I was by then seven and eight years old. Eventually I was sent to a charity institution in Florida, called the National Children's Cardiac Home, and for the first three months I was in solitary. Then they put me in a room with a couple of other kids, but for the first few months—six, eight months—I was on my back most of the time. The Florida climate was good for rheumatic children. Everybody in the place had heart conditions, and all of us were kids.

My family moved from New York to Iowa while I was at the home, and it was in Iowa that I first experienced the deliberate consequences that follow from the accident of being born a Jew. While I was at the home, I used to write my family all the time and tell them, "I can't stand it here. Let me come home." When they brought me to the institution, they said if I didn't like it they would take me back at the end of three weeks. When at the end of three weeks I told them I didn't like it at all, they said, "Well, you have to stay."

After a couple of years I did leave—I was "discharged" as they called it. I went to Des Moines, where my family had moved, and they were strangers to me. The whole thing was an act: they were making believe they were my family and I was making believe I was in the family, and it was just a matter of minutes to see who was going to break out of the disguise first, who could play the part longer. It was like outstaring somebody.

There was, even in Des Moines, a very fat girl that almost everybody could have—that guys found and took out. The trick was, you'd give her a beer. She drank before you were supposed to drink—I mean, beer is the only thing you could get in Des Moines, or at that time it was, and then you had to be twenty-one—so you found a way to get this girl (who was fifteen or sixteen) a beer and you could make out with her. She suffered from obesity and baldness, but it didn't make any difference; it was all part of getting points. You got points for making it with her. She didn't get any points: she was losing points.

I wasn't aware until much later about the point system. It's something which moves you and controls you all the more when you're not aware of it. I was Jewish and poor in Des Moines, Iowa, where I lost so many points that I was among the subtractions.

A person's self-hatred is the measure of the effectiveness of the oppressive system under which he lives. When I accepted the judgment of those around me and internalized it, I was "in my place." This is a mark of the success of an oppressive system which nonwhite races and "marginals" all have to deal with, as the first step toward becoming liberated from that system.

Now I see how, inside my mind, I separated what I thought—the dream level—from what I did.

What do I mean by "dream level"? If a movie photographer were following you around and taking your picture, recording everything, then everything he recorded would be actual; the rest would be dream. When we sleep, our dream life—once every so many hours—contradicts and puts into question the whole basis of our waking logic. If all of our waking fantasies were acted out, they would immediately be replaced by new ones.

A lot of people live as though there were no dreams —not only no dreams at night, but no dream life at all. A while ago I saw Mrs. Nixon on television, arriving in Peru, and telling the Peruvians that all of America has them in their minds and in their hearts, and the way she was talking, the way she appeared and her whole presentation, was as though there were no ambivalence, no contradictions.

I continue being interested in the question of what validates something. For example, take a couple, a boy and a girl in high school. He is on the high school basketball team, and the girl is in the sewing club, and he finds a buddy on the baseball team, or another basketball player, and she finds a home economics major, and they double date. Everything is validated, their coupleness is validated because they look at one another and see themselves duplicated. They find a thing they enjoy in common, whether it's another baseball game or a movie or a ride in the car. It's validated by somebody else's testifying to the same importance, to the same things as being significant.

IX

Notes on The Serpent

The Curses from *The Serpent*

Because you have eaten
Of the tree of which I commanded you,
Saying: You shall not eat of it,
Cursed is the earth for your sake.

Now shall come a separation
Between the dreams inside your head
And those things which you believe
To be outside your head
And the two shall war within you.

Our aim in *The Serpent* was that we should completely reunderstand the whole territory of shame, in the light of our retelling of the story. The text follows the narrative of Genesis, and is at the same time a repudiation of its assumptions. What is deeply engaging in the biblical mythology is the discovery that its assumptions are even now the hidden bases of a lot of our own choice-making. In *Terminal* there was an even more ambitious interest: to see ourselves, in the largest way, as part of the process of nature, and to see that dying is part of that process. To assimilate *that* idea—which is true as far as anyone can say anything is true—would have a really profound effect on living in the present.

You shall be made to think,
And although few of your thoughts shall exalt you,
Many of your thoughts shall bring you sorrow,
And cause you to forget your exaltation.

I think the theater could erase and repudiate the icons. It could do this by making them visible, by showing people they are the face of a body, and by showing the body of which they are the face.

You shall use your mind
Not to understand but to doubt.
And even if you understand,
Still shall you doubt.

The text gives a structure for the playing out of the story, and includes places for the company to improvise. Performing an improvisation is seldom successful without a framework to contain that which is going on in the room in a nonverbal, nonliteral way. The springboard of the improvisation is within the narrative, as in the ecstasy of Adam and Eve after the apple has been bitten. But once the actors are in the house playing out the exploration of this ecstasy, there is the other reality of people—players and audience—and here is where the delicate and mysterious encounter takes place. That encounter is not "made," but "permitted." It is not performed at that moment, but let be. It is caused neither by the actors nor by the audience, but by the silence between them.

> In the day shall you endure
> The same longing as in the night,
> And in the night shall you endure
> The same longing as in the day.
> Henceforth shall you thirst after me.

One never knows if it's the thing which changes, or one's perception of it, but something has "moved." The thing in this case is the performance: the performance is an object of contemplation. If the actor responds to his own performance with a certain kind of appreciation, he may prevent the audience from a response. If a spectator can say, "How moved the actor was!" that response doesn't let the performance move in on him. And yet the actor *must* be moved; at the same time he must disappear, as in Yeats: "Who can tell the dancer from the dance?"

I believe a person should be "moved" at the theater: something should move, something should stir, but not just the heart strings. It is the perspective he sees from that should shift.

When your children shall be found to murder,
You shall make laws.
But these laws shall not bind.

The Serpent has a very appealing tongue. He is made of five people, and you can't tell which is the tree, which are the limbs, and which is the Serpent moving about. His tongue is very striking. It keeps coming out and moving around. Eve is fascinated with him: he is trying to talk her into eating the apple, and she explains why she can't do it. She comes and she looks at him, and he says, "Is it true that you can do anything except eat of the tree?" and she says, "Yes." She says, "I am not even allowed to touch it." And they—the Serpent-men—ask her what would happen if she did touch it, and she says: "Adam said I would die." And they say: "Not even touch . . . not touch . . . not touch it!" And they recommend that she touch it, and she goes near to it, and they take an apple and touch her. They say, "Are you dead?" and she says, "I don't know." And they say, "So you're not dead! Now that you've touched it, and you're not dead, why don't you eat?" But she says,

The Serpent (1968): BACK ROW, Cynthia Harris, Shami Chaikin; FRONT
ROW, Tina Shepard, Jim Barbosa, Ron Faber, Ralph Lee, Peter Maloney

"This place, this garden, this Eden, I would be giving this up." And they say, "That's true . . . that's true that you would be giving that up, but you don't know what it would be instead, if you ate." She says, "I don't want to give it up." And then they say, "You shouldn't eat it . . . that is true . . . if you feel that you mustn't give it up . . . but you don't know what other worlds there are at all." Then they say, "This garden . . . all these plants . . . all these animals . . . were once only imagined. . . ." And then it becomes a question of wrong or right, should she do this or that. Then they say, "You should do what you want." And she says, "What if what I want is to listen to God and not to you?" As soon as Eve says that, the Serpent has won the argument: she's doing what she wants to do. It is at that point that she takes the apple—not when they are persuading her, but at the point where she has the choice—clear and open. She takes the apple, and this is the moment when she breaks the law of God as it was told to her. According to the myth, it is also the dissipation of the garden, the collapse of Eden.

Accursed, you shall glimpse Eden
All the days of your life.
But you shall not come again.
And if you should come,
You would not know it.

The point where we as a group and as individuals get involved in *The Serpent* is where the curses come. We ask: "How are we cursed? What is a curse?" A curse in this case means something which is forever, not to be reversed or modified. What do we experience that way—locked, fixed, unchangeable? We talked and talked about the curses, and out of all this Jean-Claude van Itallie constructed them. It was really a very important time for us, because whenever all of us agree on anything, it is an event.

One of the curses has God saying:

And your children shall live in fear of me.
And your children shall live in fear of you,
And your children shall live in fear of each other.
You shall be afraid of everyone else,
And you shall even be afraid of yourself.
Fear and shame are first cousins;
We are supposed to be afraid.

We did a lot of things, many experiments. I thought perhaps Adam and Eve should start by being naked, that we should experiment with this. If we are all in the garden and God says, "You are naked," how do we know what that feels like? There is a shame in nudity.

And in the end
The earth shall wax old like a garment
And be cast off by me.

101

It would be hard to overstress the importance of the group effort. The collaboration required that each person address himself to the major questions: what are my own early pictures of "first man," "first woman," "first discovery of sex," God and the serpent, the Garden of Eden, the First Murder, Cain and Abel? These questions dealt with a personally remembered "first time." They were questions we stopped asking after childhood. We had the Genesis story to ask them through.

> Accursed, you shall be alone.
> For whatever you think,
> And whatever you see or hear,
> You shall think it and see it and hear it, alone.
> Henceforth shall you thirst after me.

Finally, we stopped asking these questions because they were unanswerable (even though we gave or guessed at answers). Later we substituted "adult" answerable questions.

TO THE ACTORS PREPARING THE SERPENT—SPRING 1968

The Open Theater is a miniature government as is any group or organization. It's always difficult because there is nothing harder than actually getting along with other people, except for getting along with yourself.

Problems within groups are often pinned on certain issues and certain people, but when these issues and people are taken care of, they are soon replaced with others because it is a deeper and irrational level that is being mined. The problem is that a theater has finally to perform in some way, and performing is sharing. In our case performing is taking private work out into the world. If it were possible just to move the workshop work to audiences, it would be one thing, but it isn't. Performing takes another kind of preparation. It is giving birth, and the pain and trauma of birth is part of the move from private to public.

REFLECTIONS — SPRING 1970

In the last few months I have been thinking that maybe I don't want to stay at the Open Theater, but to do other things. Before this I've rarely felt the temptation to do anything outside the Open Theater. And I ask myself, "Why?" It's because I feel that we're stuck. We've become predictable. I'm very concerned that we won't be able to get to the basic work on *Terminal*, because people in the group feel so split up. Some of you will stay and some of you will go, and there will be many complex feelings about this that will create a lot of confusion, and we may not survive this period. I'm concerned about that; but it seems to me more important to take that risk than to go on as we have been going.

103

We are continually renaming the enemy. Sometimes the enemy is a production, because in moving
from the improvisational stage to the production
stage, there are no handrails. It's very traumatic,
all this changing. I've learned that the workshop
emphasis and the performance emphasis are completely different. At first I didn't know just how
different this was—that the actor in one kind of involvement is really not prepared for the other kind.

When the Open Theater started, we were only a
private laboratory. We did performances, occa-
sionally, but basically we were a laboratory performing unfinished work. Then with *Viet Rock*, written by
Meg Terry, we became a laboratory group performing a work which was being finished, and which,
though it did not start out that way, came to be a
commercial venture. The same thing happened with
America Hurrah, but it took longer for it to happen.
Jean-Claude van Itallie wrote the plays and brought
them in, but, unlike *The Serpent*, he did not work
them out improvisationally with the actors, but
addressed himself to whatever caught his interest in
the exercises and themes we were working on (except
for *Motel*, which he had written independently).
There was a play, and there was a producer, and
there was a commercial situation, and we agreed to do
it, and we did it.

As an actor you have a choice: you can define your-

104

America Hurrah (1966): 1st row, Ronnie Gilbert, Joyce Aaron, Jim
Barbosa; 2nd row, Bill Macy, Henry Calvert; 3rd row, Connard Fowkes,
Cynthia Harris

self in the terms you are being defined in by the critics, the audiences, or your colleagues in the theater. If you define yourself in these outside terms, you have only one course, to continue on that path you are on. I saw how difficult it was for people not to accept the classification they were given by other people. It becomes a kind of responsibility: you undertake the responsibility of being a successful person. For us there was no impetus left to do anything else, to do any research: there was not the time or the space. We were being processed as a "success."

Then *The Serpent:* starting from the beginning, we had a utopian community. It couldn't have been better: there was not one wrong current. Everyone was deferential to everyone else, and we maintained a strict, though unspoken, rule of friendliness among one another. Then with the start of the preparation for the production there grew a kind of dismay, and that dismay was carried through in every step of the actual mounting of *The Serpent.* The dismay that began at the beginning of the process continued throughout; as we came closer and closer to the point of actually performing, it really got bad. Each performance was like a confirmation of our disappointment, in spite of, or in part because of, the public success. Then we went to Europe with it, and everything was difficult: people with each other, the actors in relation to the work, in relation to me, in relation to Van Itallie. Everything was off.

Nothing was working. There was a sense of betrayal, that each of us had somehow betrayed the other. When we came back from the tour, it was a matter of whether or not to pick up the pieces.

We picked up some pieces. First, we decided not to do *The Serpent* any more, because it represented this awful period, and then we did pick it up, and we did it again, and somehow, in spite of all that, we got back into it, and really re-formed it, and strengthened it. When we performed it, it was good. We had somehow endured this very, very difficult period.

X

What you call the spirit of the age is in reality one's own spirit in which the age is mirrored.

—GOETHE

Notes from Summer 1970

It was a long story. *Terminal* has not been as difficult as *The Serpent* in terms of the interrelationships between people, although it's been very difficult from other points of view. As soon as we started work on *Terminal*, we began moving into our private responses to dying. We were telling each other stories. Tina Shephard was telling about her mother, who had cancer, and she talked about her experience of seeing her mother deteriorate and about the performance she felt herself giving as the daughter. Usually the first thing a person says when coming into a hospital is, "You look very well," or, "You look better"—to include this person in the human race again. Tina's story was about her problem in doing this. Somewhere in the story was the line "I see you (to her mother), but I don't see you dying (to us)." There was much more than that in the story, but those two

108

phrases and the particular gesture of hiding and revealing became an emblem of the story.

Right now I have a very heavy schedule and very limited energy, but still I want to do more direct and specifically political action. I have many opinions about how civil disobedience should take place, and I feel strongly that it *should* take place. For me every one of the concrete things I do, like the draft counseling, is to try to find ways in which I can subvert the system, both in me and outside.

There's a trend in today's mystical theater to say that we are divided into outer (social) and inner selves, and that the inner man is "true" as opposed to the outer one. The inner self is always alone and to itself; it is the little shapeless, bewildered man who is inside the social man, protected or rejected by the social man, but never disappearing. Because he never disappears, he is understood to be most true of all that's true. It is the ever-presentness and unmanageableness of the inner man, precisely because he is always unable to be named, managed, or assembled, which gives him a greater semblance of truth.

All this assumes that the inner man is not subject to training and re-education, as the outer man is. It assumes that the outer self is so programed that one must go inside for spontaneity. It assumes that the two selves are barely related. It assumes that only what we are unable to share is true. It assumes that what is true cannot be touched in order for it to remain true. This comes to represent the inner self as soul, voluntarily kept imprisoned by an outer self eroded by the world, and to represent the inner self as being burdened with a hopeless history of sin.

As we were in the spring of 1970, we couldn't even agree together to try to go to a prison to perform. Part of the whole experiment then included experimenting in relation to audiences and efforts in relation to performances and to circumstances which would force us to understand things we hadn't had to understand before. If we could get into prisons, if we could get into high schools, if we could get into GI coffeehouses, and if we can perform there, and if we could experience a contact with these audiences, or a failure to contact, we could say: "O.K., we haven't found a mutuality with the high school audiences, but we will try to work through the GI audiences, or we will go into the prison situation instead." The point is that if we were in situations which called for serious consideration by us, then I think we would have to look at things from a point of deeper involvement and we should come to a greater political understanding.

THE PATH AND THE BOULDER

The eyes are set in the head and part of the eye itself is facing in—the blind part, but a great part.

All the same, the seeing part is what's facing outward—seeing all the time.

If I walk a path with a boulder in the way, I walk around it—if I see it as a boulder.

A fence I might break, or also walk around.

What am I doing? Am I stylizing myself so that others can see me? Withholding myself so that others will not see me withholding myself? Am I playing at dying and sometimes at thinking?

I'm playing my play.

To the Actors: Terminal *Rehearsal*

At a certain point last year I thought I was in the last days of my life and I carried on inside my skull where nobody else could hear. I wailed, I wept, I screamed, and I died very unwillingly. I bargained with the fates, and I lied to myself again and again. You'd think that at death's door the lying would stop. Not for me.

I said to myself that I felt things I didn't feel and I bribed people for pity. I've since learned that I'm not going to die so fast; I am functioning well, and when I no longer function this well, there's an operation which may revive me and keep me alive longer still. Chances are some of you will outlive me; chances are through accident or illness somebody in this room will take off before me. There's no way of predicting any of this—but we're all here now. That's Number One. And we'll all leave this world one day. That's Number Two. We have a relationship to both of these facts about ourselves. The truth is they are as interrelated as day and night. To focus on one is to summon the other. "I see you. I don't see you dying. I see you. I don't see you living. I see you. I don't see you."

Open your eyes and look around you. Madness is in the saddle. . . . Resisting madness can be the maddest way of being mad.
— NORMAN O. BROWN

There is no principle I have held in absolute terms. Not one.

I am a pacifist. Even though I can imagine circumstances where I might contradict the pacifist position, I would uphold it ninety-five percent of the time. Because I would contradict it five percent of the time doesn't mean that I must abandon the position.

My activities which have supported this position consist of draft counseling, aiding and abetting deserters, demonstrations, civil disobedience, and other less organized actions. Being a pacifist is a position that requires continual reassessment as to how to activate it. This is necessary because it is a position against an impulse. The impulse to injure and to kill is not unnatural, any more than is the impulse to regret it.

It's my feeling that the highest human decisions any of us could take will have to wait until there is agreement not to kill each other. Even when we want to. Even when it seems right. Permission to kill is like a fence in the way of human evolution. Violence is right only for the one who survives it.

EMBLEMS

The crown is emblematic of the king. The bars are emblematic of the prison. If an emblematic part of an action is played out, with the actor living *in* the action, there is a resonance beyond what there would be if the entire action were played out. The spectator completes the action from the part of it which is being performed. The emblem becomes a meeting point for the actor and the spectator. The emblem of an action can be performed through a gesture, a sound, a word, or a series of any of these. The emblem is not a symbol which represents an action; it is made up of *parts* of the *whole* action.

LEFT TO RIGHT, Nick Orzell, Seth Allen, Joseph Chaikin

ME AND MY BROTHER

LEFT TO RIGHT, Sully Boyer, Seth Allen, Joseph Chaikin, Maria Tucci

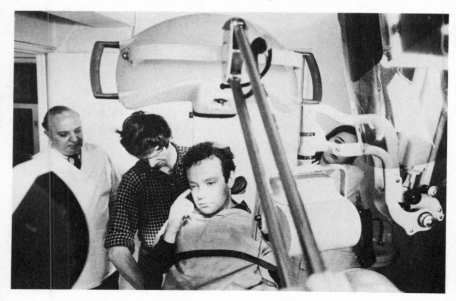

FOREGROUND, Bill Macy; BACKGROUND, Joseph Chaikin

Film by Robert Frank (1968)

LEFT TO RIGHT, Joseph Chaikin, Julius Orlovsky, Allen Ginsberg

Jamming

Storytelling, a relatively new working element with us, is a way in which we begin the exploration of new material. Each of us takes turns telling a story to the others, and after a story we try to find the emblems. The actor can be as prejudiced as he wants, for or against any character in his story. The story is made up of words, sounds, movements, and silences. The storyteller wants to have the listener make contact with the same points that he did—to see from the same subjective point of view.

Jamming is the study of an emblem. If we have an emblem, "I see you, I don't see you dying," the jamming becomes a kind of contemplation of that emblem. The term comes from jazz, from the jam session. One actor comes in and moves in contemplation of a theme, traveling within the rhythms, going through and out of the phrasing, sometimes using just the gesture, sometimes reducing the whole thing to pure sound, all of it related to the emblem. Then another comes in and together they give way and open up on the theme. During the jamming, if the performers let it, the theme moves into associations, a combination of free and structured form.

We started jamming in *The Serpent*, with the five men who made up the serpent. Before that we had been jamming with sound alone; beginning with *The Serpent* we began to include meaning and intention. An actor can jam with himself, as Joyce Aaron did in the line "What was given to me was impossible to work with." When she went into jamming, she found it became something like: "What was given to me what was given to me was what was given to me was impo was impo was impo," etc. By doing this she showed that there is a very great amount of inner material and music to draw from while staying with the same intention and words.

To the Company, 1970: Acting and Action

When I have worked in agit-prop theater, the main intent was to make points to the audience—to inform . . . to arouse . . . to preach. After a few performances the actor becomes like a barker, immune to his own shouting. Soon the hollowness which he feels becomes part of his presentation.

Propaganda theater carries with it a trap of falling into one-dimensionality. For me the most effective political theater has been the kind where the audience and performers have a direct communal relationship; for example, the New Lafayette Theatre in Harlem, Teatro Campesino performing for workers, and the

Women's Collective Theater perform in a context that heightens and intensifies the theater experience. The Bread and Puppet Theater performing at a demonstration both enhances the gathering and is enhanced by it. Political theater for general audiences seems only to throw more opinions on the already overloaded heap of opinions. At the Open Theater we experienced the greatest political contact while playing in institutions such as prisons.

Theater can operate to alter perception in ways other than direct political action. It can create a way of seeing that in turn can aid human transformation. In addition to being aware of economic factors, political theater can be in touch with the subjective and mythological dimension of the people for which it is a voice.

What could be done to support an overthrow of the government? I believe this question is partially answered by the aim of moving through a change of perception with the audience. When you see differently, both you and that which you see has changed. Meanwhile, continually putting into question the context of performing (lower ticket prices, or free admission if possible; audience to come from where? Who will profit? etc.) and continually aiming at a collective situation within the group can promote a living response to the oppressive system under which we live.

How can we support a revolutionary voice and

avoid serving the capitalist machine, without depriving ourselves of doing this work we love? There is no need to demand that material we work on must have topical propaganda benefit any more than we would demand that every poem written should be against the State and every song sung should be a call to action.

In our own generation extreme forms of ego-gratification are culturally supported. . . . Arrogant and unbridled egoists as family men, as officers of the law and in business, have been again and again portrayed by novelists and dramatists, and they are familiar in every community. Like the behaviour of Puritan divines, their courses of action are often more asocial than those of the inmates of the penitentiaries. In terms of the suffering, the frustration that they spread about them there is probably no comparison. There is very possibly as great a degree of mental warping. Yet they are entrusted with positions of great influence and importance and are as a rule fathers of families. Their impress both upon their own children and upon the structure of our society is indelible. They are not described in our manuals of psychiatry because they are supported by every tenet of our civilization. They are sure of themselves in real life in a way that is possible only to those who are oriented to the points of the compass laid down in their own culture. Nevertheless a future psychiatry may well ransack our novels and letters and public records for illumination upon a type of abnormality to which it would not otherwise give credence. In every society it is among this very group of the culturally encouraged and fortified that some of the most extreme types of human behaviour are fostered.

—RUTH BENEDICT

A quality which I've seen in common among the most extraordinary people I've known has something to do with risk. Some part of a person's interior which is generally concealed and protected is instead exposed to the world. It's an inner life which they can't or won't cover over.

Anybody not busy being born is busy dying.

—BOB DYLAN

At this point in time nothing which is not severe is respected. Dogma and fanaticism claim the greatest admiration. What is gentle is thought to be weak.

Hymn
Let there be peace on earth
And let it begin with me.

120

JOSEPH CHAIKIN

If our wishes, feelings, desires, hopes, fears, perception, imagination, dreams . . . do not correspond to the law, they are outlawed and excommunicated. Outlawed and excommunicated, they do not cease to exist, but they do undergo secondary transformations. . . . The way to get a person to do what you want him to do is to give an order. The way to get a person to be what you want him to be is to tell him he is that or to tell someone else in front of him that he is that. This is a form of social hypnosis. . . . We are instructed to be honest, but instructed to operate in our experience in ways that can only be called dishonest. . . . "What may be put into words or what words may be put into" . . . We are taught that what our teachers say is true. We are taught to think we are wrong if we can't see that they are right. One tries to narrow the credibility gap, between what one cannot help but see going on and the story that is told by invalidating one's own senses.

—R. D. LAING

X I

The Murder

The murder of the beast takes place. For some it's
a sport: it comes to self-defense. If I don't kill this
beast inside me, *it* may kill me. Who am I? Well, I
am the one you address when you talk to me nicely,
when we understand each other—what you hold me
responsible for. That's me.

How come you don't notice the slaughter? Because
it's what I have to do alone. There are those things a
person must—can only—do alone. I take the beast
home and there I carefully pick the room for slaughter. It's not in the living room. I want no stains and
no ghosts there. Each thing in the living room must
validate and confirm each other thing. I go to the
cellar alone with my beast and I slaughter him. I go
by myself and I commit the slaughter by myself. I
leave him there nearly dead. I hear his grunts in my
ear as I walk upstairs. Having begun, I return again
and again to the cellar to keep his wounds from

closing—from healing. He knows me and watches me do it.

This cellar is a private place. No one else knows the passage. The beast is my private matter. Only he knows I slaughter him and he has no memory of what he was before my first swing of the ax. He never dies and he never stops bleeding. He has little nourishment and still he doesn't die. I know that because he stirs.

Now he no longer recognizes me when I come downstairs, and I no longer remember the first time I struck him.

More Notes on Myself

There are experiences you have in your life: the before and after things, when you are not quite the same after as you were before. Something is included, or something is taken away, or something is added: but it is definitely before and after. I had such an experience with my heart.

Before my doctor did the diagnostic operation, the night before, the two who were going to perform the surgery came to see me. This is customary at the hospital: they come to the patient and introduce themselves, so that you don't think of them as an extension of the machines they are using, but as people who are using these machines. (The operation would take five hours, during which time I had to be awake.) And one of them said: "As we're doing this operation, we'll have the radio on, and we'll talk to each other. One of us will say to the other one, 'Did you see the papers this morning?' and the other will make some comment saying what he saw in the papers." They actually told me what kind of conversation they were going to have the next day so that I would invalidate what was happening to me physically.

In the morning they took me down, and I'd been frightened before in my life with different kinds of fear, but this was special. I'm lying in the room, and the people are running around and doing things. There were a tremendous number of machines, and, unlike what I had expected, they didn't look very modern; the paint was old on them, and they didn't look like those metal and silver things you expect, but like old things they were still using. I said—as though from another person in me—I said: "How do you get a tube all the way from my arm—all the way up to my heart?" And the doctor said: "Oh, the tube's a very skinny tube. It's like spaghetti." The way they put things was always to make them not serious and casual.

They had the radio program, and then one started: "Did you see the paper this morning?" And the other said, "Yes," and at that point, I couldn't take it any more. I assumed, or took for granted, that they knew better than the patient where the head's supposed to be, because they've had experience before. Then I broke down. I just completely broke down. My body was throbbing and sobbing and screaming. I really didn't want to; I wanted to impress them as a kind of stoic, but I had lost myself already. I had wanted to assist them.

I felt then, in the clearest way I have ever felt, something that I think goes on all the time. I felt it then especially because my body was pinned down: it was the sense of the two extreme ends of me, the person as terrified as I ever remember being, and the performer making the right words and trying to form the responses that would register in that room.

When I began to break down, when I was experiencing that feeling that was bigger than my body, at first they tried to disregard it, as though it wasn't happening. But when I started to go up and down like a yo-yo, and it was clear that I was not going to be this quiet thing to work on, then they called for some "in" word for morphine—I asked him later what it was and he told me—and the nurse gave me a shot of something. And in my head I felt: it doesn't matter what she gives me, this feeling is so deep and so intense, nothing is going to neutralize it. She couldn't have found the chemical: it doesn't exist. You come to this point of despair and you say to yourself: There is absolutely not one way in the world to accommodate this feeling. It doesn't fit; I can't fit it in any part of me, under the ribs, in the middle of the head, there is no place for it. It absolutely doesn't fit; it can't be contained.

The tears of the world are a constant quantity. For each one who begins to weep somewhere else another stops. The same is true of the laugh. Let us not then speak ill of our generation. Let us not speak well of it either. Let us not speak of it at all. It's true the population has increased.

—BECKETT

The medical-economic reality in this country is emblematic of the System which literally chooses who is to survive. I renounce my government for its inequitable economic system. When I get sick, I really have to worry if I can pay my medical bills. When I need medicine, which is constantly, I have to work this through, and I renounce it because other people who have fewer advantages than I have don't even have the choices I have. They have no way in which they can work it through. I renounce its defining for me my experience. I renounce the person it intends for me to be.

XII

Deep in What Sleep?

> *. . . we can indicate by language why language cannot say what it cannot say.*
>
> —R. D. LAING

Realms —Winter 1971

My own work in theater has taken me into commercial entertainment where the effort goes into figuring out what the customer will buy. I have also been into "specialized" New York theater and professional schools. I have been a part of satirical theater, and later agit-prop theater. I have gone from the theater of de-mystification to the theater of mystification. In my present stage, the work I'm doing is without classification. If I could classify it, I would drop it.

As part of my work in theater, I've come to understand that any theater brings with it *systems of perception*. Each kind of theater is itself a satellite which orbits around a corresponding life mode. Theater styles are interrelated with living and thought styles. Each man-made object which we see carries within it a recommendation to be seen within a given system of perception. Frequently, a confusion makes one look even at natural objects in this way.

The terms *realms, levels, modes,* are all ways of trying to define a territory of experience without necessarily giving a name to the definition, because once you give it a name it is no longer the same. I think of realms as being like radio stations. In music the realm is both the key and the dynamics in which it is played. In Bach's *St. Matthew's Passion* the narrative is the continuity and returning point, but within the narrative are stops where, for example, a violin comes in with a contralto voice singing contrapuntally about grief and sin. Then the narrative returns. During the duet between the violin and the contralto, the music calls on the listener with a special form of intimacy. One way we realize this realm is through contrast with the narrative.

In the song, "Good Vibrations," sung by the Beach Boys, they move from one to another to another realm and key within the song. Structurally, this is clearer to understand in music, but it is no less present in acting.

JOSEPH CHAIKIN

A Raid on the Inarticulate

The original impulse, in the Open Theater, was to get away from talking, and in doing so we were mostly rejecting our own training. In speaking for the stage there are usually two directions: one, talking "natural," just like you and me—which our Method training had emphasized; and two, talking "beautiful," the King's English, borrowing from the British speech and passing it off as musical, cultural, theatrical—as our classical training had taught us. To one degree or another these are the only two ways of talking I found in American theater, and these kinds of emphases are completely inadequate.

In the fall of 1968 we began an intensive study of speaking which lasted about ten weeks. All the voice and speaking work followed from that initial study. Previously, our interest had been to get away from language altogether, to go into talking as mumbling, talking as singing. We began an analysis of words as sound, words as meaning, and words as intention * of the speaker. As we began this work, there was a trap at every corner. To work on speaking, we had to go back to breathing and voice. There the trap

* By intention I mean the active signal sent from one person to another. On a given line, for example, you could say "Hi!" One "Hi!" is to welcome you, and the other "Hi!" could be, "How come you're so late?"—the same line taking on different intention.

against working simply was the pressure we felt to "beautify" the projected sound of the actor. Working on meaning and nonmeaning, the trap was to make everything meaningless. Working on the intentions of the speaker, the trap was to focus on the available "characters" and the clichés of those characters, such as the Brooklyn switchboard operator, the broad showmanship of the priest, the proselytizing politician. In other words we found here, as with each new thing that we've begun, a tendency against discovery and toward confirming the cliché. Once we became aware of this tendency, we resumed a serious inquiry into intention, meaning, and sound.

Each person's voice is already adequately developed to convey intention within a very limited range. We can be understood when we say "pass the salt." We can be heard when we shout down the block. It takes perhaps five weeks of practice to enable the voice to project more loudly, ten weeks to deepen it, and maybe fifteen weeks to bring more resonance to it. It takes a whole re-education of the voice, however, for breathing and vocal sound to be in touch with parts of ourselves which are as yet unformed.

Everything that takes place is in us. The voice of the tortured as well as the voice of the blessed. We need to liberate the sounds closed up in us. Ultimately, acting is to be able to speak in the tongues of the tortured, assassinated, betrayed, starving parts of ourselves imprisoned in the disguise of the "setup." And to locate and liberate those voices which sing from the precious buried parts of ourselves where we are bewildered and alive beyond business matters, in irreducible radiance. Work on the voice is a balancing between very specific technical disciplines and mysterious areas having to do with breathing rhythm and space. The voice and sounds which make up a single word or phrase can allow both the speaker and listener to enter into precise meaning and experience. Instead of being only a flat label, the spoken word becomes three-dimensional. As a group, I feel that experiments with words and vocal sound may be our next major involvement. Only words have such precise and focused meaning; working with them represents an element of our work I would like to deepen and advance.

We've just begun a study of breathing rhythm— voice independent of words and voice applied to words. We've scratched the surface now enough to know that the study holds a vast and affirming exploration yet to come.

I've worked with the deaf, where I've learned about the experience of breath as sound moving through the body without benefit of ears. This experience is basically the same for hearing people when we go more deeply into the question about breath and sound. The body is like the pipe in an organ through which the wind moves, causing the sound, and requires that the whole inner space be open and clear.

The spoken word is too often simply giving sound to the printed word. We should want to find how to speak words, not simply as data, but using the sounds which make up the word to create the universe of the word. For example, if the word "radiance" can be spoken not simply to stand for the *idea*, but to bring up "radiance," then the voice is creating through the word. The question is how to use the voice, not to refer to a condition, but to enter it.

The whole area of spoken language is occupied territory. We can only find a way to free speaking through patient, long exploration and discipline. We need to find how we can sing words and bellow words and pray words and crush words. I'm very eager to get on with this study, because I know that there is so much that we can yet discover.

At what points in the performance is the spectator likely to tune out and go into a space in his own mind, forgetting about what is going on onstage? A Buddhist monk reminds the people who come to him that "thought is only thought, but very often people think that what they are thinking is actually taking place." A person may have a full response to a thought; once the thought leaves, the response may stay; the person may not even be able to trace his response from the thought.

It's only by virtue of our eyes that there are stars.
—BERTRAND RUSSELL

JOSEPH CHAIKIN

Notes on Forming Exercises

Exercises are very important. When I can envision
a kind of behavior, a kind of ambiance, a kind of in-
terrelating, a kind of environment, a kind of physical
life, and kinds of sounds, then, if I find the proper
exercise, I invite the actor to inhabit that realm. The
exercise will surely be different from what I first
thought it might be, because what happens is always
different from what's planned. Between me and the
actors that which has been transformed from idea
into action becomes the meeting place.

EXERCISES

At the Open Theater I have gone though periods
of inventing exercises which I thought to be highly
creative. Now I see that I was confusing variety
with development. Among the many exercises I
devised were a few which had value to us as a group
at that time. If I had been less concerned with volume
and could have refined the valuable exercises and
deepened them, we would have gained more individually and as an ensemble. Instead, we created a
gymnasium. Ironically, the glib exercises from that
period of work are the ones which are now most used
in schools and rehearsal outside the Open Theater.

An exercise breaks the existing premise within a

133

group and opens up what is seemingly fixed. There
is no aspect of work among groups concerning performance and audience, or having to do with training,
which canot be studied through an exercise.

When a group of people are beginning to work on
an already existing text, exercises can be formed
to enter the material. Exercises can be created to
locate the world which the writer has designated.

In acting, training exercises for body, voice, and
concentration can be the means through which the
actor develops. Exercises can also detour development. For example, a dance exercise may be good for
the dancer, and an actor can sometimes gain strength
and agility through dance, but it shouldn't be confused with body exercises for the actor. The same is
true of singing exercises.

I believe that any work for the theater, any different company about to do the same work, and even different actors within the same company require a
different approach. There is no path laid out beforehand. The exercises, discussions, and relationships
within the group and toward the material must be
newly assessed at the beginning of each new adventure
of work. Among the particular people who use them,
exercises are used to develop a particular direction.
In books which document exercises, I feel that I am
reading a book of recipes, whether they are exercises
by Stanislavski, Viola Spolin, or the Open Theater.
The reason they cannot be documented is because it

134

is an internal territory. If the actor could explain it, the exercise would be unnecessary. The exercise is an agreed-upon structure. The structure can be explained yet it is empty of content. An exercise is untranslatable.

If you can't explain what you mean, it doesn't mean you don't know what it is, or that you don't mean it. It only means either that *it* can't be explained or that *you* can't explain it.

In Brazil a boy brought his foreign friend home to meet his mother. The mother knew only Portuguese and she didn't know there was any other language, and she didn't know that everybody would not understand Portuguese. The mother talked to her son's friend in Portuguese. When she saw that he didn't understand her, she talked louder.

I cannot say what cannot be said, but sounds can make us listen to the silence.

R. D. LAING

Beckett often has an alarm clock in his plays; in *Happy Days* as well as in *Endgame* I have often thought the alarm clock was to wake the audience up in a certain way, to bring them back to attention when they were just about to go to sleep.

I think that Beckett writes from a place where he is absolutely alone. There is no consolation. There is nobody around to hold your hand; only a few jokes.

It is only ideas of such colossal proportions that a symbol for them cannot be created—that are vague and intangible and brooding, incomprehensible, and fearful—that produce madness. . . . Her thinking is wild—but I have the wilder idea that if I can force her to keep it hitched to a pencil, and hold it down to the slow rhythm of writing things out in longhand —the practice might tame her somewhat. . . . Anything that can be whittled down to fit words—is not all madness.

—LARA JEFFERSON

136

XIII

You're on Earth. There's no cure for that.
—BECKETT

Notes on Playing Endgame

In playing *Endgame* one comes to know Beckett in
a way that is a special way of knowing somebody.
When you go into the world the writer makes, something happens; you are living through his world
even if you are acting. His world acts on you. It enlarges you. It reduces you. It mechanizes you. I feel
that you come into a kind of union with that writer,
which comes to be like a permanent friendship. It
doesn't matter if you ever meet the person.

I most admire a writer who goes where it's almost
unendurable, and still survives. I feel that Beckett
does that. I feel I have been able to go to that place
he lives in. Playing *Endgame* was the second time in
my life I felt very glad to be acting. The other time
was playing Galy Gay in *Man Is Man.* Beckett and
Brecht: it is as though you had two very great friends
whom you wouldn't necessarily think to invite to the

same party: they might not get along, or they might not find in each other what you found. There is no particular reason to mix them. It is a special relationship I feel to both of them; one is dead and the other alive.

There are many realms in *Endgame*. One that is very explicit is that of the performer doing vaudeville for the audience. The audience is in the theater, the performer is on stage: this is a reality of the theater. The actor, as performer, entertains the audience by doing routines.

Then there is the level where the actor, as a person, is talking to each of the people in the audience, as a person, on that level where each is absolutely and completely alone. Times like when Hamm says: "One day you'll be blind, like me. You'll be sitting there, a speck in the void, in the dark, forever, like me. Infinite emptiness will be all around you, all the resurrected dead of all the ages wouldn't fill it."

There is the "talk from the heart," another level which returns again and again: where the one character says to the other, "Do you think we are beginning to mean something? Maybe then it won't all have been for nothing!" At the end of the play Clov is talking about heart feelings when he says, "the earth is extinguished, though I never saw it lit."

But nothing stays. Everything, everything turns again into the realm of the performer, the audience, and the show. Even when one says to the other, "Do

Endgame (1970): LEFT TO RIGHT, Joseph Chaikin, Peter Maloney

you believe in the life to come?" he only replies, "Mine was always that."

On the Audience

One of the baffling questions for the actor is "Who is the audience?" Is the audience (as in films) a group of individual spectators each dreaming the action in a dark room? Is the audience a number of people who are each potential rescuers to the action, the drowning of a civilization? Is the audience made up of anonymous intimates who are being signaled by a spy who's been with the enemy? Or is the audience a group of people wanting the relaxation of an entertainment—to be comfortably purged, fascinated, or amused? Should the audience be addressed as fools or saints? Every performer makes some decision about the audience in his own mind: personalizing, making specific the anonymous. He makes a secret choice, in the course of events, as to "who" the audience is. In attributing a particular quality to the audience, one invites the participation of that quality. Who is he secretly addressing? The casting agent present in the audience? The critic who could advance his career? His parents? The ghost of Gandhi? His greatest love? Himself? The same action addressing each of these

140

has in it a very different message. To whom does the actor personally dedicate his performance?

EXPECTING; DEDICATING;
LEVELS OF ADDRESS

An actor playing in a soap opera is working within a specific style. This style is informed by a mythology invented out of a particular view of living. If the actor acting in the soap opera doesn't examine the life view to which it relates, the actor is less likely to see his own relationship to the character. All the connections start to collapse from there. This style, the way it is approached, and the way it is intended to be perceived—this is what I refer to as levels of acting.

When you expect something, you leave that which you expect free to happen. Expecting a thing, you are calling it up; calling it up, you are making an open place for it to come in. You call on something in another which is also alive in yourself.

In the fall of 1966 we began a number of exercises, the first of which was our *Midsummer Night's Dream* series. We began with the idea of the audience being composed of trees, squirrels, tables, and chairs, and gradually we moved from the idea of an inanimate audience to an audience of human beings. The idea was that we were always addressing ourselves to someone or some element or some force. The idea is to select it. I call up a thing or a person and I *dedicate* what I am

141

going to do. I say to myself that I am playing this performance for—let's say, Martin Luther King, Jr. Now the Martin Luther King I am playing it for is not the one who is talked about in the papers, out of whose assassination movies are being made. What is involved is my own relationship to Martin Luther King, who has in some way imprinted himself on me. You choose a person with whom you are connected, as though an electric wire was running between you, and you say: for you, to you, in honor of you, I dedicate the next two hours. I may forget you as I am going through it, and I may consciously return to you; it may be nothing more than the gesture saying "I'm doing it. I don't know what my dedication to you will do, but I address you and share this time with you." The scope of the dedication is limitless.

The dedication can be to Martin Luther King, Goebbels, Caesar, de Sade, Antigone (the person needn't have actually lived to be a living connection to you), Che Guevara, Simone Weil, Billie Holliday, Buddha, Nietzsche, Spinoza, Mephistopheles (if he can be actualized for you), Anwar Sadat, all those who killed themselves, all those who murdered their sisters and brothers, all the landlords who trick their tenants, all those who are in the last weeks of their lives and know it, all those who have been resurrected (any metaphor that can be a visceral reality), all prisoners, all those who have been drowned in floods during their last moments alive, fire itself, distance,

142

or light. Any person, persons, or condition where there is a living contact.

The active part of this process is the level of address. "I've chosen the one to whom I'm dedicating this performance. Now on what level do I address him? On what level am I meeting him? The first step, that of dedicating, is choosing, closing in on a place of contact between you and another. The next thing is: what level of me do I summon in order to summon the other, so that we meet?" That level is the performing level.

That level becomes the level of meeting the audience. What we *expect* in the audience is the same as what participation we invite from them. It is your own contact that calls on and finds the level, because this is the only part that has the authority. Your own cynicism calls on the cynicism in the audience; your own clarity calls on the clarity in the audience. Since each person in the audience, like each actor, possesses so many different levels, you as actor are not imposing a level but rather locating one. In that sense the audience is made into yet other actors.

If I pick someone who isn't a whole force, then that dedication will be circular, a private affair between me and myself, me and my memory playing off each other. But if what I pick is representative of what I feel is in each person in the audience, as well as being specific and subjective to me, then I don't have to turn away from the audience, but the audience makes the dedication possible. I'm working with *this* audience, with this particular living level of my meeting place with Martin Luther King. I say to myself, in working with them, that it is his spirit, his energy, his aspiration, his agony, his persistence which is in everybody: I go on and do the dedication and it brings me to a different level. It changes my behavior in a way that I welcome, because it permits me to be enhanced, to be changed by the connection with this person.

I have often found, with actors, that dedication takes them away from a certain self-consciousness, or that it has suspended that expectation of appreciation. The audience tends to become stereotyped in the mind of an actor, and what the dedication does is to invite a particular presence from the audience, and unfix that stereotype. It is very hard for us to get away from the wish to be applauded—to charm and seduce the audience. An actor is organically dedicating the performance, whether he is aware of it or not. What we are doing is guiding the dedication deliberately.

NOTES ON PERFORMING
"ENDGAME" IN PRISON

Roberta Sklar and I had wanted for some time to experiment with audiences who would be fundamentally different from the ones we were playing for. In the spring of 1970 the first real opportunity came when we were asked to perform *Endgame* before the prisoners at Grasslands Penitentiary. The warden of the prison has to approve everything which is performed before the prisoners, and so Roberta, who directed the production, sent him a copy of *Endgame*. Seeing no harm in it, he agreed to let us do it.

My impressions of the performance itself are those of a blind man: playing Hamm, I cannot see, but I can hear and feel the quality of the room. At this time we were not using a curtain for the play, and so we had to be ready in our places before the audience came in. We got set up, I took my place in my chair and was covered with an old sheet. The room was quiet; all the prisoners were waiting downstairs. Suddenly, they were permitted up. It was their Friday night activity, and they were very raucous. The feeling was very much like being at a burlesque or a circus: something one looked forward to very much, with no obligation to be any special kind of audience, but only to be entertained. The prisoners were very physical with each other: it was like Friday night dates, and anybody could be the date of anyone else. I was able to observe this later, when we met them, and I was told that it went on during the play as well—they were leaning on each other and touching each other the way people do in a movie on a date.

Then the house lights dimmed, and the light came up full on stage. Usually when that happens, the hum in the audience—restrained to begin with—goes all the way out. You can feel the sound following the lights, as the audience takes its cue. But here there was very little difference in the noise: they kept the same thing going.

Clov starts the show, and when Peter Maloney came on and started his thing, they thought he was a riot. And he shifted his performance right away to suit what was happening.

I had no idea how to start in with the "Can there be misery loftier than mine?" line, because it was on a different key. I went ahead and did it, and I felt the prisoners' immediate indifference to my character and their waiting until Peter returned. Then Peter came back on, and they became interested in my character from the point of view of one who is giving orders to Clov from the villain, the warden. This was a situation in which perhaps five of the prisoners had been to the theater before, so the majority of them made up a virgin audience. They had undoubtedly all been to the movies, but the movies they had seen had probably been no preparation for Beckett. The warden was in the audience, and the audience was surrounded by guards with firearms. Once I became identified as the warden, the prisoners watched the play as a kind of tennis game, rooting for the one character and hissing the other. Once in a while I found them interested in a sympathetic way with Hamm, but usually I remained the villain.

146

When the old couple came on, they saw this as the essence of man and woman, as the absolute essential interaction; they saw it in nostalgia, in irritation, in misunderstanding. They thought it was hilarious, and they responded to everything that could be taken as sexy—and you could hardly call any of it sexy—as though it were a strip tease. They articulated what they felt about: there was nothing that they didn't cheer, laugh, boo, sigh, or make some response to. During the play there were occasional announcements from the loud-speaker. I would hear: "The clinic is open and anybody who needs medication should leave now, and come down immediately." That announcement was made about three times, and each time you would hear prisoners leaving, each prisoner being escorted by a guard.

Then the play was over, and we were able to talk to the prisoners. Some of them said, "What's it supposed to be about?" I am used to that question, and I never answer it. I always try to shift the question, to see what *they* saw it to be about—about a prisoner and a warden, about the revolution, or about the impulse toward revolution and its being crushed. I spoke to about six of them, and then, suddenly, the loud-speaker came on again: "All right, time for cell lock-up. Leave two at a time and stay visible." The noise was over, silence came into the room, and they left, two at a time.

We had a few minutes, to be social with the

staff, the warden and the guards, but the social didn't take off at all, because we stayed completely segregated. The warden walked around, trying to talk to us; the guards sat at one table and we sat at a different table, and we didn't say anything to each other. One guard said, as we were leaving, "Why don't you bring another show around, one with some music and some girls?"

I felt that the play had impressed itself on the prisoners very much. The prisoners knew that the warden had to approve each thing they saw. And one of them, knowing the warden had read it, said to me: "If he had known what this play is about—if he had *really* known—he would never have let you do it."

Since then we have learned much more about prison life. In the 1970–71 year we performed *Terminal* in many minimum- and maximum-security prisons on the East Coast and Canada. These experiences have made a very great change in us. A change that we are acting on, and will continue to act from. We have moved to a sense of full solidarity with our sisters and brothers in prison.

XIV

If you think something is "true," no matter how obscure that "truth" seems to be and no matter how specific to you alone, somewhere, someone else thinks it now and at a different time someone had already built a monument to it.

Nothing is so fatal to an ideal as its realization.
—SCHOPENHAUER

Without the military, the world political leaders would just be doddering men arguing obsolete ideas about power. One of our first aims is to dissolve the military.

Nightmares come and go—the dream remains the same.

A critic I know told me once that he wrote a review, read it over and, because he had a deadline, submitted it as it was, but he was aware that he could just as easily have written another kind of review altogether. He had at least fifteen contrary responses to the same thing, and this was simply the first one that came out.

Useless
To judge that this layer of life is more important than another,
That the outside of the earth is better than the inside,
And the blanket less important than the towel, except
In the cold.

The question contains the answer in it.

A yoga exercise. Concentrate on an object and its association.
Keep bringing your attention back to the object; then another object. Then think, who is the "I Am" who is concentrating?

I have to judge you to know where I stand.

The equation goes like this: the greater the dissent of the governed, the greater will be the violence of the government.

—GEORGE JACKSON

150

Alternatives

There is no longer any given action to take in response to a given condition. A civil-rights demonstration in Washington . . . a sit-in against escalation . . . a shoot-out . . . a rally . . . an essay . . . an occupation of a building. There is no one general antidote for any one type of problem. What is difficult is that we have to create the action that we are going to take. The action is not at hand. Within the circumstances of a particular hierarchical condition lies a particular possibility for action, which may not destroy the condition but could render it meaningless and illegitimate.

At the time of this writing there are things in New York City which meet the challenge of today's stress. In meeting the challenge and not drowning in the malaise of fraud and lunacy, these things triumph: The Alternate U, WBAI, WIN Magazine, Bread and Puppet Theater, the Fortune Society. These living cells are encouraging to me in the sense of *giving courage.*

Unless all existence is a medium of revelation, no particular revelation is possible.

—WILLIAM TEMPLE

151

There are things (circumstances) which must cause
you to lose your reason or you have none to lose.

—LESSING

Laughter is a collapse of control in response to
something which can't be fitted in the file cabinet of
the mind. It is a form of ecstasy, a collapse of reason
into a basic clarity.

The Balance in Groups

I've worked with and observed a number of groups.
One of the things that strikes me is that within one
group some people are growing and some people
stay in one place, and some seasons bring out the
one and some the other. The one who stays in one
place has a great power within a group because at
all times he is able to identify where he is and where
he was. The one who's moving is always somewhat
lost because he's not at a place he can clearly define.
He's between a place he knew, and moving to where
he doesn't know. To move from one known place to
another known place is not really to move at all.

In a group the balance of forces between the one
who is still and the one who is moving is perhaps
always greater on the side of the still one. In this

152

Mutations (1972): LEFT TO RIGHT, Joanne Schmidman, Tom Lillard, Tina
Shepard, Raymond Barry, Paul Zimet, Ellen Maddow; KNEELING, Shami
Chaikin

circumstance the director must find a way to encourage the one who's evolving even if he is evolving beyond the director.

When criticizing an actor in what he does, the director must first understand what the actor thinks he is doing.

TALENT

There is no way to develop talent, only to invite it to be released. It's a mysterious gift, no more equally distributed than bright sunny days over a year.

The teacher of the actor is like the teacher of small children. He looks for the right steps for each student, and when the student is about to make his discovery, the teacher must disappear. If the teacher looks for his own satisfaction at the point of discovery, the student does not fully discover. Take a child who has a pile of blocks but can't find a way to make what he wants out of them. If the teacher guides him in making the shape the child wants to make, he should disappear when the child is about to take the definitive step. By taking this step himself, the child discovers his own thoughts.

In the development of an actor, the teacher tells the student that if he continues to study in this direction, he will come to the point where he will recognize when he is performing truthfully. The teacher has already fixed what is true beforehand. The student hasn't. Eventually, the student only learns what is true for the teacher.

Critics

Once a reviewer matures and has won himself an audience for his productions in print, he is called a critic. At this stage he will probably most appreciate works which sanction and encourage his own life style and direction. At this stage the critic also becomes known to those who perform, and they speculate about his attitudes in advance. This speculation becomes major business. The established critic has become part of the economic establishment.

I have rarely known a case where a critic's response to actors, directors, or writers has expanded or encouraged their talent—I *have* known cases where by panning or praising, the critic has crushed or discouraged creative inspiration.

Measuring creative situations amounts to processing them as a commodity. The commercial critic performs a useful function to the mercantile theater, and the intellectual critic duplicates the commercial critic on a smaller scale, because he too forces the artist into a competitive arena where there is no possible benefit.

The theater is, as it is, not only because of who is in

it doing what, but because of what the critics are permitting to be done, and by whom.

To the Actors, Spring 1970— The Breakup of the Group

This is the end of a chapter. It is like a kind of marriage: there is much habit and shared responsibility and history that makes you not want to end it, but gradually, through more than a year of work and practice, this phase of our work has been ending. I am glad we have had this time, and I'm glad that it is over.

Over the weeks, months, and years as I have watched actors in workshops and in performances, I've come to notice patterns forming and breaking. For these few weeks that are left, there are still traps we may fall into and also windows we may be able to open. We have come to learn that the world cannot be shut out; we must examine the world within ourselves so that we can understand the way in which it is dictating our choices. It's been a rich and a dense time we've had together.

We in the Open Theater are parts of a structure that for one reason or another is no longer capable of growth. By structure I don't mean a physical, legal,

156

or business framework—this has never had an important effect on us. The real structure is unexpressed, a subjective quantity made up of many invisible rules and tacit promises. Within this structure, at this point, all we can do is maintain the status quo; that's not good enough.

Notes on the Re-forming
of the Group—Fall 1970

In September 1970 a new group began under the name of the Open Theater. The Open Theater is only a name, a label, that a group of people who planned to meet regularly gave themselves several years ago. We began as a study group; later we performed dark nights at the Sheridan Square Playhouse. *America Hurrah, Viet Rock, The Serpent, Terminal, Endgame;* evenings of political theater called "masks" followed. Through all these stages of public work, the Open Theater was used as a name, even though different people were involved in different projects. Some, like Peter Feldman, Barbara Vann, Lee Worley, and Jim Barbosa, were part of the work from the beginning; others joined in during the period beginning with *The Serpent.*

With each crisis and collapse of an outmoded structure, the group became more and more sharply focused. The present company of actors are: Ray Barry, Shami Chaikin, Tom Lilliard, Tina Shephard, Joann Schmidman, and Paul Zimet. This present group has come closer to being a truly developing and working collective. Continuity is essential for growth in the theater. A writer or painter can work alone and establish continuity by living his life and enduring his failures and successes, but the collective effort of theater requires a special continuity in order to grow.

To the Company—Spring 1971

Now we're at work on *Mutations,* our newest work. We're dealing with human mutation, with ourselves as mutations, contemplating the human form we haven't taken, on the experience of being torn away from ourselves. Working as part of this group is like having several sets of eyes, not just my own. I have felt the deepest and most sensitive collaboration during this period, and I hope we will be able to focus clearly enough and to move beyond the obstructions so as to be able to bring into this work some of what we are discovering together.

It's exhilarating to work together through this confusion, toward some kind of clarity. As a group

158

Mutations (1972): LEFT TO RIGHT, Tom Lillard, Shami Chaikin

I'm never sure how long we will survive; endurance probably isn't the best criterion anyway. The more baffled and astonished we permit ourselves to be, the more we discover and learn. After *Mutations* I will be moving in a completely different direction, still looking into the theater event, and in the process continuing to change my relationship to it. Where that will take me I don't know.

To the Reader—February 1972

After putting aside for a while the notes that make up *The Presence of the Actor*, I have just taken them up again and reread them. In many cases there are statements that appear to me unjustified or in need of more explaining. I will resist this. I can only say that my life and my views change radically from one period to another; as I feel detached from old views, at some time in the future I will probably feel separated from much of what is written here. This winter has been a changing time for me: a crossroads. In a way I wish that I could begin the book again, but instead, *The Presence of the Actor* will have to stand as what I called it when we started—notes from several levels of myself. The struggle continues, and my work will continue to be shaped by it. There won't be another book, but I will try to keep in touch from time to time about the shape of some of these changes.

The best answers are those that destroy the question.

—SUSAN SONTAG

JOSEPH CHAIKIN was born of Russian parents in Brooklyn, New York in 1935 and grew up in Des Moines, Iowa. After attending Drake University he returned to New York City and joined the Living Theater in 1959, receiving three *Village Voice* Obie awards for acting, most famously for his performance of Galy-Gay in Bertolt Brecht's *Man Is Man*. In 1963, he founded the Open Theater, an influential laboratory/workshop for actors and playwrights, celebrated during its decade of existence for such collaborative productions as Megan Terry's *Viet Rock* and Jean-Claude van Itallie's *The Serpent* and for its powerful presentation of Samuel Beckett's *Endgame*, in which Mr. Chaikin played Hamm. Disbanding the Open Theatre to prevent its institutionalization, Mr. Chaikin directed numerous productions at home and abroad, appeared in the title role of Georg Büchner's *Woyzeck*, led the Winter Project in the creation of *Re-Arrangements* and *Tourists and Refugees*, among others, and collaborated with Sam Shepard on the solo works *Tongues* and *Savage/Love* (published in *Joseph Chaikin and Sam Shepard: Letters and Texts, 1972–1984*). In 1984, during his third open-heart operation, Mr. Chaikin suffered an aphasic stroke which has severely affected his use and comprehension of language but which has not diminished his desire or capacity for ongoing theatrical experimentation. Recent efforts have included highly-regarded productions of Eugene Ionesco's *The Bald Soprano* and Beckett's *Waiting for Godot* as well as performances of *The War in Heaven* and *Struck Dumb*, post-stroke studies of aphasia written in collaboration with Shepard and van Itallie, respectively.

In addition to his Obie awards for acting, Mr. Chaikin is the recipient of two Obies for direction, the first Obie award for Lifetime Achievement, a Drama Desk Award, a Vernon Rice Award, two Guggenheim fellowships, honorary doctorates from Drake University and Kent State University and the Edwin Booth Award.